The Tran

'*Time Reveals Truth*' *by François Lemoyne,*
from the Wallace Collection in London

Used by kind permission of the
Trustees of the Wallace Collection, London

THE TRANSFORMING POWER OF PRAYER

From Illusion to Reality

Michael Marshall

continuum

Published by the Continuum International Publishing Group

The Tower Building, 11 York Road, London SE1 7NX

80 Maiden Lane, Suite 704, New York NY 10038

www.continuumbooks.com

First published 2011

British Library Cataloguing-in-Publication Data

A catalogue record for this book is available from the British Library.

ISBN 978-1-4411-1724-3

Typeset by Kenneth Burnley, Wirral, Cheshire

Printed and bound in Great Britain

Dedicated with gratitude to

The SPA Fellowship
(**S**cripture, **P**rayer, **A**ction)
Friends and fellow travellers on the spiritual journey

But when one turns to the Lord, the veil is removed. Now the Lord is the Spirit, and where the Spirit of the Lord is, there is freedom.

And all of us, with unveiled faces, seeing the glory of the Lord as though reflected in a mirror, are being transformed into the same image from one degree of glory to another; for this comes from the Lord, the Spirit.

(2 Corinthians 3.16–18)

Contents

Acknowledgements

All quotations from scripture, unless otherwise indicated, are taken from the New Revised Standard Version of the Bible. Frequent references are made to *The Message* Bible, a translation in contemporary language by Eugene Peterson. Its use in this book needs no justification. Eugene Peterson's remarkable use of language, as readers will discover, gives new life to familiar texts.

From the outset I wish to express a real debt of gratitude to Father Thomas Keating, founder of the Centering Prayer Movement and of Contemplative Outreach. His writings and conferences have inspired many people throughout the world – clergy and laity alike – to press forward on the spiritual journey, with particular reference to the disciplined practice of Centering Prayer. I am also most grateful to the Revd Soon Han Choi, my co-founder of the SPA Fellowship – a small prayer fellowship, exploring together the spiritual reading of scripture ('lectio divina'), and personal and corporate centering prayer with its outworkings of discipleship and action in daily life.

For novices, computers are both a curse and a blessing for the authors of books. I have experienced many traumas in the course of producing this book, including at one point the theft of my laptop! However, countless telephone calls for help were readily and generously responded to by Roy Hyslop, without whom I doubt very much if the book would ever have been completed. Also, I should like to acknowledge with gratitude all

ACKNOWLEDGEMENTS

the encouragement I received from Robin Baird-Smith of Continuum, who from the outset helped me to bring together much that lies behind the writing of this book.

Bishop Michael Marshall
October 2010

INTRODUCTION

The Spiritual Journey from Illusion to Reality

Every picture tells a story

'Time Reveals Truth' by the relatively unknown French artist, François Lemoyne, in the Wallace Collection in London, is a large and most striking painting. I knew immediately on the first occasion I saw it that, in order to relate further to it, I needed to know something more about it and perhaps even a little more about the artist. A nearby attendant was most helpful.

The painting shows an old man with a long scythe in his hand. He is thrusting it towards the heart of another man lying on the ground in the foreground of the painting. In the extended left hand of the man whose heart is being pierced, is a mask which he has snatched painfully from his face. At the same time, he is holding up his other hand in an attempt to shade his eyes from the bright light streaming from the old man with the long scythe. Wrappings and clothing which had clearly covered up most of the man's body are falling away, threatening to leave him naked. The old man with the scythe in one hand is rescuing and holding a young and somewhat beautiful, naked maiden in his other arm. In the distance is the shadowy face of yet a third man who is withdrawing into the gloom and the darker background of the picture.

However, it is the story behind the painting that I found especially fascinating. The man with the scythe, as I was later told, is intended to depict 'Father Time'. The young maiden being

1

rescued by 'Father Time' personifies naked Truth. The man in the foreground whose heart is about to be pierced by the scythe, with his extended left hand, is tearing off the mask of his false self behind which he had always hidden, but from which at last he is compelled to reveal his true face and his true self, though clearly close to death as he does so. He is holding up his right hand to cover his eyes and to shield him from the blinding light issuing from the rescued naked maiden. The face receding into the background, according to the artist's declared intention, is supposed to represent that of 'envy'.

But that is not the whole story. 'This was the very last painting that François Lemoyne ever did,' said the informative attendant. 'The very next day, after the artist had completed this painting, he committed suicide!'

Of course, I cannot pretend to have any inside knowledge of the motivation for the suicide: the painting tells its own story, and perhaps that is sufficient. It struck me at the time, however, and even more forcefully the further I reflected on the painting, that it presents us with something of a challenge. How reluctant we are, throughout our lives, to reveal to the world – let alone to ourselves – our true selves: our persistent refusal to remove our masks together with those outer impressionable wrappings in which we both dress up and cover up, and with which we seek so often to impress the world at large. For masquerading is the name of the game – the games people play, hiding behind the masking cosmetics of the facade we want to show to those around us. However – and here is the pain in all of this – in the process of casting aside our masks and our false selves, in order to give place for the true self and for our real identity to emerge, we necessarily experience a kind of 'death', either figuratively or literally.

For what is old simply cannot accommodate the new, any more than falsehood can be the bedfellow of truth. Christ himself spelt out this eternal truth when he spoke of the impracticality of putting 'new wine into old wineskins' (Matthew 9.17).

2

(Presumably something of this is what St Paul consistently wished to communicate when he spoke so persistently about the need for 'dying to sin' – that death of the old, false self.)

Then again, as the painting also depicts, it's that persistence of the old, false self which drives us to envy and covetousness: the nagging desire and longing to be some other person with their perceived wealth, good looks, successful career or their apparently superior lifestyle. This over-identification with an imagined alternative identity so often results in the rejection of our own, true and unique identity. We go through life in the shadows of illusion, rather than in the light of true self-knowledge. For only the truth and the self-knowledge of who we are, as well as who we are not, can set us free to become who we were truly created to be.

The transforming power of prayer

From start to finish, this re-creation of the true self is the work of God in whose mind and heart we were first imagined. Our part in this lengthy, and at times painful process of transformation, is to open ourselves in prayer and to consent to God's continuing work in and through us – perfecting what he first began. We need to know, however, that this process of re-creation – being 'born again', as the scriptures put it – is essentially a long and exacting process, as layer after layer is removed to reveal the truth, which alone can set us free. That process of transformation is the principal theme of this book.

'Time will tell,' as we say, 'and the truth will out.' Therefore, however painful this process of transformation may be, we all need – sooner, rather than later – to come to terms with the fact that ultimately the truth will be exposed in the light of a new day, when all will be revealed. Christ is quite explicit about the fate of all 'cover-up' and counterfeit, especially in the name of religion, warning his disciples to beware of the 'leaven' of hypocrisy. 'Nothing is covered up that will not be uncovered, and nothing secret that will not become known. Therefore whatever you have said in the dark will be heard in the light, and what you have whispered behind closed doors will be proclaimed from the housetops' (Luke 12.2f). On a further occasion, Christ remarks that although 'light has come into the world', the successors of Adam and Eve to a man and a woman 'prefer darkness', or at the very least the illusory shadows of comfortable and cosy half-truths. Yet all spiritual progress, as demonstrated in the rite of Christian baptism, with the giving of the lighted, baptismal candle, points to the journey 'from darkness to light' as true disciples reflect the 'light of Christ' and themselves, in turn, shine 'as lights in the world to the glory of God the Father'.

Most poignantly, however, for me, was that scythe, with its implied image of harvesting, depicted as reaching into the heart of the man on the ground. As I remained looking at the painting, the uncomfortable words from the epistle to the Hebrews welled up: 'Indeed, the word of God is living and active, sharper than any two-edged sword, piercing until it divides soul from spirit, joints from marrow; it is able to judge the thoughts and intentions of the heart. And before him no creature is hidden, but all are naked and laid bare to the eyes of the one to whom we must render an account' (Hebrews 4.12f).

Truth and freedom belong together

So, as Jesus said, 'If you continue in my word, you are truly my disciples; and you will know the truth, and the truth will make you free' (John 8.31f.). He added: 'So if the Son makes you free, you will be free indeed' (John 8.36). St Paul endorses this link between truth and freedom – between freedom and the Truth that Christ claims to be in his own person. 'For freedom Christ has set us free' (Galatians 5.1).

The spiritual journey or the way of discipleship clearly marks out the road to that freedom from the bondage of illusion and the false self. The 'Way' is clearly marked out for us. It is Christ alone who, as he himself claimed, is the 'Way' to the 'Truth' that is truly 'Life'-giving. It is Christ and Christ alone who sets us free from the bondage of fear, engendered by that false self – living, as perhaps we do, with the persistent fear that one day our cover will be blown and that when the 'Masked Ball' is ended and as the light of dawn breaks, all masks must be cast aside.

Prayer as the work of God within us

In retrospect, I think it was no accident that that particular picture caught my attention so very powerfully on my first visit to the Gallery. For, to me, the fascinating factor is not so much that I *saw* it, but rather that I *noticed* it, and perceived its immense power to resonate with something deep within me. I'm somewhat fearfully aware that there is something almost 'autobiographical' in the story behind the painting. This book attempts to outline a similar story to that depicted in the painting. For the spiritual life, as we sometimes say, or the spiritual journey as I prefer to speak of it, invites and frequently even demands a willingness to open up to God's living Word – the Word made flesh in the person of Jesus – who speaks to us *through* the words of scripture, if only we will turn aside to listen and to receive that word deep within our hearts and our inner-most selves. ('O that today you would listen to his voice! Do not harden your hearts' (Psalm 95).) A true understanding and practice of prayer, when it is perceived and received as God's work in us and what he is doing for us through his Holy Spirit, rather than what we are seeking to do for him, undoubtedly has the power to transform us and to release us from the seductive illusions of that false self which has been conditioned, both by nature and nurture, since the day of our birth.

Growing in prayer – from saying prayers to prayer

For many faithful Christians – laity, even leading laity on Church Councils or in Synods as well as clergy and pastors – prayer, whether personal or corporate, gets stuck and ceases to develop and mature from little more than just 'saying prayers'.

> Prayer is something more than an exterior act performed out of a sense of duty, an act in which we tell God various things he already knows, a kind of daily attendance in the presence of the Sovereign who awaits, morning and evening, the submission of his subjects. Even though Christians find, to their pain and sorrow, that their prayer never rises above this level, they know well enough that it should be something more. Somewhere, here, there is a hidden treasure, if only I could find it and dig it up – a seed that has the power to grow into a mighty tree bearing abundant flowers and fruits, if only I had the will to plant and cultivate it. Yet this duty of mine, though dry and bitter, is pregnant with a life of the fullest freedom, could I once open and give myself up to it. We know all this or, at least, have some inkling of it, through what we have occasionally experienced, but it is another matter to venture further on the road which leads into the promised land.[1]

If anything of those words of von Balthasar resonate with the prospective reader, then perhaps this book might be for you! The book attempts to open up a further way of prayer beyond merely saying prayers. It is a representation of the traditional practice of the spiritual reading of scripture ('lectio divina' as outlined in Appendix A), preparing us for the deeper wordless and silent prayer of the Holy Spirit leading us on from Centering Prayer to the grace of Contemplative Prayer (as outlined in Appendix B). It is in the practice of the reading of scripture in this way that we move on into the wordless and silent prayer of the heart – Centering Prayer or Contemplative Prayer. I must confess that for much of my ministry I had assumed, quite wrongly, that such prayer was exclusively for professionals – monks and nuns – and not for general-practitioner clergy like myself, let alone for lay people. The challenge of this book, in the words of von Balthasar, however, is to encourage *all* Christians to 'open and give ourselves up' so that we might 'venture further along the road that leads to the promised land'.

A road less travelled

The spiritual journey is a journey into a new awareness and self-knowledge, received through an ever deepening knowledge and love of God who reveals himself to us through the work and prayer of the Holy Spirit within us. Slowly, as we travel along that road, we are changed, as the Spirit of God brings about re-birth and transformation, and in which knowledge *about* God grows into knowledge *of* God in an ever deepening and intimate relationship *with* God. And then, like that scythe in the painting by Lemoyne, the sword spoken of in the epistle to the Hebrews, 'the inner thoughts and intentions of the heart' are revealed: that false self, conditioned since our birth and from the early years of our formation, whether by family or by the prevailing culture and inborn attitudes and prejudices of our environment – engendered even by our 'religious' environment.

Gently yet persistently – and always by grace and grace alone – we are enabled to hear that voice of him who calls us out of the darkness and shadows of illusion into the glorious light of reality and freedom as the children of God. For such is our true identity and who we truly are. Yet all this must be undertaken by faith, since it is not at all clear at this stage, nor is it yet revealed, what we will look like when the Spirit of Love and Truth, in the course of time, has finished working within us (1 John 4). All we know in the course of our journey into God, is that when Christ is finally revealed, each of us uniquely will reflect the likeness of Christ as sons and daughters of the living God, by adoption and grace, in what can appropriately be termed 'a family likeness' to the divine. Then and then only will we finally be released from the addictions and compulsive behaviour-patterns and programmes conditioned both by our former nature and nurture. 'So if anyone is in Christ, there is a new creation: everything old has passed away; see, everything has become new!' (2 Corinthians 5.17).

This book is about that journey from the old to the new; from the false to the true; from illusion to reality. The writing of it, however, is undertaken with some necessary diffidence. I feel a little like that travelling salesman seeking to market hair-restorer. He arrives on the doorstep of a potential customer and is invited to 'come in' and talk further with the prospect of an imminent sale. However, as he enters the house and politely takes off his hat, he loses all credibility, let alone the possibility of a sale, as he reveals the visible and contradictory evidence of his own, totally bald head!

So God forbid that I should give the impression of being far advanced on the new life journey, let alone, in any sense, having 'arrived': arrival at the finishing-post is most definitely not in this world, even for the greatest spiritual athletes. It takes far more than the mere passage of time to ensure maturity: people do not inevitably improve with the passing of the years – far from it. The latest is not necessarily the best. Such a view is what C. S. Lewis perceptively termed 'chronological snobbery'! Yet . . .

> however mixed our motives in writing (or reading) books, in the end they are about our desire to share (and learn more about) what it means to be human and what matters to us most, our desire 'to speak what we feel, not what we ought to say'. For those who write such books, and nervously launch them into a critical world, they aim to be, in short, a small – and sometimes quite risky – act of love.[2]

Notes

1   Hans Urs von Balthasar, *Balthasar on Prayer* (Geoffrey Chapman Ltd, 1961), p. 11.
2   Michael Mayne, *The Enduring Melody* (Darton, Longman & Todd Ltd, 2006), p. 246, quoting *King Lear*, Act V, Scene iii.

1

Keeping Up Appearances

Illusion and reality

William Blake, the eighteenth-century mystic, poet and artist, claims that 'we are put on earth a little space, that we may learn to bear the beams of love'.[1] In many ways, that telling remark sums up the whole purpose of Christian discipleship or the spiritual journey. Yet, our persistent response to Blake's perceptive and challenging claim throughout the pages of human experience has been very ambivalent at best and, at worst, totally dismissive. On the one hand, the human story consistently records a deep longing to be drawn into the bright 'beams' of an unconditional and unending love, a seeking and a searching for God or for a deeper reality for our lives, often referred to as a spiritual yearning. Yet, on the other hand and at the same time, humanity exhibits a fearful resistance to that which such an uncompromising exposure to the bright 'beams' of truth and love inevitably demands.

Perhaps T. S. Eliot is more on target when he concludes that 'human kind cannot bear very much reality'.[2] He was not the first to make that assertion. Such an insight is reinforced in the claim of Christ himself, that although the light of life and love have come into the world, 'people loved darkness rather than light' (John 3.19), or at least a life in the shadows and the half-light in which illusion and self-deception thrive – all the more easily masquerading as reality.

And so it is that Christian discipleship or the spiritual journey should be seen as a journey or pilgrimage – the journey of a lifetime – in which we travel from the 'shadowlands' of illusion (as C. S. Lewis referred to life in this world) to the bright 'beams' of reality in that heavenly city, where there is no need of 'lamp or sun, for the Lord God will be their light' (Revelation 22.5). From the outset, therefore, we need to know that such a journey will demand a radical transformation of lifestyle as well as a change of direction, if we are to move from our culturally conditioned comfort zones of an illusory security into the uncharted and multidimensional world of reality and ultimate maturity. Little wonder that most of us, most of the time, undertake such a demanding journey of exploration into the unknown with a measure of reluctance, frequently looking back – two steps forward and one step back – repeatedly and even obsessively running for the shelter of all kinds of escape devices, so as to hide from the searching 'beams' of a ruthless and challenging reality.

The externals of religion

Our greatest ally in this whole illusory exercise is, of course, the devil himself – that arch deceiver – promising us the freedom to 'do our own thing'. Yet contrary to what we might expect, the devil's most fruitful sphere of activity is whenever and wherever we are at our most 'religious', and, most conspicuously of all, when we are out on the road of what we might like to refer to as our spiritual journey. It is not insignificant that Christ himself encountered the most devilish delusions when praying in the wilderness. At face value, the three temptations in the wilderness were plausible enough and not least if Jesus really were the Son of God. In that case, then surely would it not reasonably follow that the devil's suggested miracles would be little more than an 'in-house' job? And notice, the devil even quotes a text from scripture to support his case. But then, as scripture should remind us, the devil is supremely the angel of darkness who delights to masquerade as the angel of light – the prince of lies and empty promises. So where better can the devil promote his programmes of illusion and delusion than in the environment of religion? Paradoxically, it's here that the devil is amazingly so at home!

In every age it's all too easy for the external forms of religion to flourish, while in reality lacking the inner drive and the power to accomplish what, to all outward appearances, they would appear to effect. Experience should tell us that the counterfeit in all walks of life frequently passes off as the real thing, at least in the short run, and always more convincingly when in the shadows of illusion and delusion. Yet, in the long run, it is time and the course of time, if nothing else, that will eventually reveal truth, as the painting referred to earlier seeks to portray.

On the spiritual journey, therefore, we need to pray at every turn in the road for the spirit of discernment if we are to distinguish between illusion and reality. We do this best when we understand prayer primarily as that which God does, rather than what we do. True prayer is primarily a response to God's initiative in loving us with a love which in turn creates within us a deep yearning and longing to respond in kind. If, however, we seek to take the initiative, there will always be the danger that we present a 'religious' side of ourselves when coming to pray, both in the content of our prayer as well as in its assumed 'religious' language.

> Real prayer is utterly truthful. This is what makes it hard. We have to be there before God as we really are, maybe upset, angry, worried, emotionally at sixes and sevens. This is the self I set in God's loving gaze; this is the little creature he loves and has to deal with.[3]

There is certainly nothing cosy about such prayer as it seeks to bear those 'beams' of love, truth and reality. For such prayer, originating in the heart of God himself, teaches, corrects and informs. It is when we are open, silent and receptive that, with the 'ears' of our hearts, we are able to hear the truth that frequently we would rather choose not to hear!

Distinguishing between things that differ

In the course of our spiritual journey, illusion and reality are often so close that our vain attempts to distinguish between appearance and reality come across as little more than quibbling. Part of the difficulty is that illusion and reality, like love and hatred, are not at opposite ends of the spectrum: on the contrary, they are frequently next-door neighbours, living in the closest and apparently comfortable proximity. Therein lies their power to confuse even the most analytical probing. At times they are so extraordinarily similar in appearance and so close as to give the appearance of being almost identical.

But 'close' in what sense: by distance, or by approach? For there is a real difference and a distinction that needs to be made – albeit one that is frequently unperceived – between something that is 'close' in the sense of similar in appearance (that is, close by *distance*) but which, on further examination, turns out to be radically different, or indeed the very opposite, by *approach*. In reality, however, the two proximities and likenesses are as different as light from darkness and as illusion from the bright beams of reality, truth and love.

So perhaps an analogy may help to make clearer this distinction between nearness and closeness as measured 'by distance' in contrast to that as measured 'by approach'.

Let us suppose that we are doing a mountain walk to the village which is our home. At mid-day we come to the top of a cliff where we are, in space, very near it because it is just below us. We could drop a stone into it. But as we are no cragsmen we can't get down. We must go a long way round:

five miles, maybe. At many points during that *detour* we shall, statically, be far further from the village than we were when we sat above the cliff. But only statically. In terms of progress we shall be 'nearer' our baths and teas.[4]

Jesus himself makes this distinction between nearness and likeness 'by distance' as opposed to nearness and likeness 'by approach'. So he said of one of the scribes who had been questioning him, honestly and with insight, that the scribe was, *by approach*, 'not far from the kingdom of God' (Mark 12.34). Similarly with some of the sinners and tax collectors. By 'distance' they would undoubtedly give the impression and illusion from outward appearances of being a long way *by distance* from, and not even remotely like, the citizens of the Kingdom. Paradoxically, however, and *by approach*, in real terms and in the light of true discernment, Jesus perceived them as being closer to the Kingdom than the religious leaders of the establishment, with their outward appearance and semblance of religiosity and the keeping of the law.

Perhaps even more telling is that similar contrast that Jesus draws between the Pharisee and the tax collector who went up to the Temple to pray (Luke 18.10). The prayer of the Pharisee gave the appearance, illusion and form of being religious and the real thing – what most people would expect from the lips of a religious leader. Yet from the perspective of the Kingdom and in the eyes of Jesus, and furthermore in reality, it was the tax collector and not the Pharisee who, by his 'approach', in real terms, got to the heart of the matter – in a word, 'repentance'. So it is that the tax collector is affirmed by Jesus as being closer to God and his Kingdom *by approach* than the Pharisee with all his outward displays of religious fervour and pious observances.

So much of the teaching of Jesus in the New Testament is given over to this distinction between outward appearances of religiosity and the inner reality of true religion – between piety and true spirituality – and not least in his incisive teaching on prayer. So many of the cautions of Jesus in his Sermon on the Mount clearly contrast the external appearances of religious practices, with an authentic development of the inner life of the Spirit. So for example, almsgiving should not be heralded with a 'trumpet call'. As for the cosmetics of fasting with 'dismal' and even 'disfigured faces', that is remonstrated against by Jesus as being blatantly 'hypocritical' – as literally putting on the play-actor's mask. 'Beware of practising your piety before others in order to be seen by them; for then you have no reward from your Father in heaven' (Matthew 6.1). For, as scripture reminds us, in the words of the Lord to Samuel the prophet, God does not look on outward appearances or 'the height of his stature . . . for the LORD does not see as mortals; they look on the outward appearance, but the LORD looks on the heart' (1 Samuel 16.7).

The inner life of prayer

For Jesus, personal prayer and the spiritual journey are essentially perceived as the inner and hidden work of the Holy Spirit. 'And whenever you pray, do not be like the hypocrites; for they love to stand and pray in the synagogues and at the street corners, so that they may be seen by others . . . But whenever you pray, go into your room and shut the door and pray to your Father who is in secret' (Matthew 6.5, 6). It is only in solitude and in the silence and hidden, inner 'chamber' of the heart that God reveals himself to us, and rescues us by the indwelling action of his Holy Spirit from the illusions of piety or religiosity.

Throughout the Gospel narratives, Jesus in his personal prayer to his Father and ours, frequently retreats to the hills and to the solitude and silence of the hidden hours of the night or the early hours of the day, for that 'quality time' with God. As the psalmist puts it: 'For God alone my soul waits in silence' (Psalm 62.1). It is only in the inner silence and in the depths of our true selves that Christ reveals the true identity of God and removes the veil that obscures his true nature from the eyes of the world. For 'no one has ever seen God. It is God the only Son, who is close to the Father's heart, who has made him known' (John 1.18).

Hence true prayer is literally a matter of 'heart to heart'. However impressive the earthquake, the thunder or the fire, as recognized locations of God's activity, Elijah needed to learn the subtle lesson that God was not *in* such outwardly impressive exhibitions of power or spiritual firework displays. Rather, God delights to be revealed only in that 'still, small voice' in the inner silence of the heart – an inner chamber into which God longs to be invited and welcomed. It is then and there that the Spirit of God teaches us and brings to our remembrance the living words of Jesus as he reveals his true identity – an identity in stark contrast to all those false projections which are resourced from our own imagination and from such knowledge as is gained through the intellect or derived from the cultural, religious conditioning of our environment and upbringing.

> But where is and what do we mean by 'the heart'? The heart is where sadness, joy, anger and other emotions are felt, here in the heart. Stand there with attention. The physical heart is a piece of muscular flesh but it is not the flesh that feels, but the soul; the carnal heart serves as an instrument for these feelings, just as the brain serves as an instrument for the mind. Stand in the heart, with the faith that God is also there, but *how* he is there we do not speculate. Pray and entreat that in due time, love for God may stir within you by his grace.[5]

Inside out and outside in

We also need to give attention to that teaching of Jesus about the 'washing of cups, pots, and bronze' on the outside, as opposed to the inner cleansing of the heart. 'Do you not see that whatever goes into a person from the outside cannot defile, since it enters, not the heart but the stomach, and goes out into the sewer? . . . It is what comes out of a person that defiles. For it is from within, from the human heart that evil intentions come' (Mark 7.18–21). Indeed, the enemy is within!

In all of these and many other instances, Jesus is not attacking the actual practices of almsgiving, fasting, prayer or the rituals of cleansing in themselves. Rather, he is pointing out the dangers of such practices and such man-made traditions, when they substitute, or, even worse, when they masquerade as ends in themselves. So Christ would urge us to see all these 'religious' practices – and not least the practice of prayer – as ways of bringing us and opening us to Christ who alone can reveal to us the true face of his Father and ours, as best we can bear this over-riding reality. So true prayer is essentially and primarily the activity of God before it is ours – the Holy Spirit praying within us. Furthermore, it is only such prayer that has the power to change and transform our lives, albeit always from the inside out, and not the reverse, and in this way rendering all religious 'cosmetics' redundant. So the psalmist prays: 'Create in me a clean heart, O God, and put a new and right spirit within me' (Psalm 51.10).

It follows therefore that in true prayer we are listening far more than speaking, if we are really seeking an encounter with the true God rather than with our projected images of God. Jesus himself cautions about using many words when we pray, for many words tempt us to suppose that, the more we speak, the more likely it is that our prayer will be heard and answered on our own terms. 'When you are praying,' said Jesus, 'do not heap up empty phrases as the Gentiles do; for they think that they will be heard because of their many words. Do not be like them, for your Father knows what you need before you ask him' (Matthew 6.7–8). First and foremost, as we shall see later, it is the 'ears of the heart' which need to be attuned to the decibels of God's first language which, paradoxically, is that of silence.

Put it another way: a heart must be really listening, really wanting the truth, really wanting God. The difficulty is that we do not want him. We want our own version of him, one we can, so to speak, carry around in our pockets rather as some superstitious people carry around a charm.[6]

What a comfortable, cosy God that sort of God is. He makes no demands and fits into our way of life, accommodating our foibles and underwriting all our culturally conditioned prejudices. In such prayer,

we can hold endless loving conversations with this one, feel we have an intimate understanding with him, we can tell him our troubles, ask for his approbation and admiration, consult him about all our affairs and decisions and get the answer we want, and this God of ours has almost nothing to do with God.[7]

Institutionalize that approach to prayer and to religion in general, and, on the grand scale of many established and powerful religious bodies such as we see today, it is not long before religious wars and conflicts are fuelled by such a God who is seen predictably to be 'our God' on 'our side', and ready to slay all those who do not conform to our view of the sort of God that they suppose God to be.

For the temptation of 'keeping up appearances' while running also to our contrived hiding places is always likely to be endemic among all those who would seek to practise 'religion' as a thing in itself, rather than as faith in a personal God who has chosen to show us his real face in the Jesus of history as well as the Christ of faith. For, as Paul Tillich wrote, 'Jesus came to save us from religion.' Such a warning is as relevant today as when it was first written against the backdrop of the ideological wars of the last century.

When Bartimaeus was healed by Jesus and regained his sight, it's Mark who pointedly tells us that the blind man first deliberately threw off his cloak before he caught his first glimpse of God in the face of Jesus (Mark 10.50). In true prayer, the 'cloaks' of evasion and illusion must be cast off, leaving us exposed to the bright 'beams of love' and truth. 'Prayer, if it is real, is an acknowledgement of our finitude, our need, our openness to be changed, our readiness to be surprised, indeed, astonished by "the beams of love".'[8]

O God, you desire truth in the innermost heart; forgive me my sins against truth; the untruth within me, the half-lies, the evasions, the exaggerations, the lying silences, the self-deceits, the masks I wear before the world. Let me stand naked before you, and see myself as I really am. Then, grant me truth in my inward parts and keep me in truth always.[9]

Notes

1   William Blake, 'The Little Black Boy' from *Poems Selected by James Fenton* (Faber & Faber Ltd, 2010), p. 9.

2   T. S. Eliot, *Murder in the Cathedral* (Faber & Faber Ltd, 1935), p. 69.

3   Sister Ruth Burrows OCD, *Essence of Prayer* (Burns & Oates, 2006), p. 88f.

4   C. S. Lewis, *The Four Loves* (Geoffrey Bles Ltd, 1960), p. 13.

5   Theophan the Recluse, *The Act of Prayer: Orthodox Anthology* (Faber & Faber Ltd, 1966), p. 191.

6   Burrows, *Essence of Prayer*, p. 14.

7   Burrows, *Essence of Prayer*, p. 14.

8   Thomas Merton, *The Climate of Monastic Prayer* (Foreword by Douglas V. Steere) (Irish University Press, 1969), p. 14.

9   George Appleton, *Daily Prayer and Praise* (Lutterworth Press, 1962).

2

The Crisis of Identity

Hide and seek!

Originally, according to the Judeo-Christian tradition, Adam and Eve were created not only in the image of God, but also in the likeness of God. Subsequently they were tempted by Satan, the prince of lies and counterfeit, to grasp with a covetous and envious spirit at being like God, their Creator – a likeness they wrongly perceived of in terms of control, power and self-esteem. However, they were deceived, and the 'likeness' which they now assimilated and attempted to copyright, predictably resulted in a total caricature and the very opposite to that of God's true nature and likeness. 'Though they knew God, they did not honour him as God or give thanks to him, but they became futile in their thinking, and their senseless minds were darkened. Claiming to be wise, they became fools; and they exchanged the glory of the immortal God for images resembling a mortal human being' (Romans 1.21f).

If, as the second-century Bishop of Lyons, Irenaeus, says, 'the glory of man is the vision of God', then it follows that once our vision of the true God was obscured, the true glory of humankind was lost and, subsequently, humanity became a pale shadow and a caricature of its former self, no longer reflecting, as it had formerly done, a true likeness of God.

However, having lost all resemblance to any true likeness of God, the haunting and subliminal *image* of God remains. God has left his indelible mark and imprint deep within the human psyche – deep and hidden from our consciousness, our senses or our intellect. The image of God, however – albeit 'smudged', to use the analogy of Gerard Manley Hopkins – stubbornly remains deep within us with a love that will not let us go. The well-known analogy of St Paul is that of a darkened and distorted mirror which necessarily no longer reflects a true image. 'We don't see things clearly' is the rendering of this well-known passage by Eugene Peterson. 'We're squinting in a fog, peering through a mist. But it won't be long before the weather clears and the sun shines bright!,' or, as St Paul puts it, when we shall see him 'face to face' and 'know, as we are known' (1 Corinthians 13.12).

Only the true features of the face and image of Christ, who alone 'is the reflection of God's glory and the exact imprint of God's very being' (Hebrews 1.3) can reveal to us the true likeness as well as the undistorted image of God. 'Whoever has seen me has seen the Father' (John 14.9) are the reassuring words, not only in answer to Philip's enquiry, but indeed to all who earnestly wish to seek a true knowledge of God. At the same time, God's self-disclosure of his true identity as revealed in the face of Christ enables us to rediscover our own true identity, as children of the one heavenly Father and as brothers and sisters of Christ, his beloved Son.

Back again to Adam and Eve. Their rejection of their true identity as creatures, snatching as they did at 'equality with God', especially in terms of the identity of the Creator, by eating from the tree of the knowledge of good and evil, has confused identities, both divine and human, ever since. The serpent had promised in the mythological truth of story-telling (incidentally, still one of the best ways for universally communicating truth), that their eyes would be opened and they would '*be like God*' (Genesis 3.5).

Such is the radical diagnosis of our human identity crisis – rooted as it is in the solidarity of our human, illusory identity of being 'like God'; that is to say, as being in ultimate control, claiming that control for ourselves and grasping it, as of right. Therein lies the fundamental and ultimate delusion of the whole human race. For, far from the eyes of Adam being opened and being able to know God and to see God as he really is, Adam's vision became distorted and seriously impaired. Both the roll-on effect as well as the fall-out from that catastrophic error of judgement are still clearly in evidence on every page of our human story. The record of history is littered with DIY demi-gods, from Herod to Hitler, all alike claiming some divine power and infallibility; and nearly always, paradoxically, such tyrants and dictators – to a man as well as to a woman – are incredibly superstitious and 'religious'.

That impaired vision of Adam and Eve, resulting from what we term 'the fall of man', meant that they could no longer relate to God as he truly was because they could no longer see God as he truly is. So Adam and Eve did what we all do: they projected onto a blank screen, subtitled 'God', their own homespun image and caricature of what they supposed God to be like – namely, an enlarged mirror-image of their own distorted and disorientated selves. So when the serpent promised that they could be 'like God', the god they sought to be like bore little or no resemblance to the true God. All the supposed characteristics which they now attributed to God in their attempts to be Godlike were out of kilter – off-centre at best, inverted and distorted like the mirror image of themselves as they had become: Adam, a self-made man, worshipping his maker!

It follows therefore that the basic flaw rooted deep within our humanity, persistently surfaces in our vain attempts to play at being God – that is, playing at being the sort of God we wrongly imagine God to be. Having been created in God's image, we have recreated God in our distorted and limited vision of who he truly is, replicating on an enlarged screen a blown-up version of that image. So now we're wrong on both fronts – both, what it is to be truly human, as well as what it is to be truly divine.

'Where are you?' the Lord God enquires as he comes in the evening to the Garden of Delight to seek out Adam who has run into the bushes and gone missing. Adam's response has been echoed down the ages in every language under the sun. 'I was afraid,' replies Adam, 'so I hid myself.' (Adam and Eve, embarrassingly self-conscious in their nakedness, we are told, had sown fig-leaves together and made themselves loincloths.) So the fashion industry began with its obsession with outward appearances, marketing a costly cover-up job! 'Keeping up appearances' becomes the name of the human game at every level, in which the false self or the illusory ego is projected and the true self is hidden and cloaked beneath many protective layers. The game of 'Hide and Seek' has gone on ever since, with God doing the seeking and the human race continuing to hide.

That story of Adam and Eve is my story, and indeed the story of the whole human race. Adam and Eve reinvented themselves into what Thomas Keating calls 'home-made selves'. The human race has been trapped in that fundamental delusion ever since.

We are thrust because of circumstances into the position of developing a home-made self that does not conform to reality. Everything entering into the world that makes survival and security, affection and esteem, and power and control our chief pursuits of happiness has to be judged on the basis of one question: Is it good for *me*? Hence, good and evil are judged not by their objective reality, but by the way we perceive them as fitting into our private universe or not.[1]

The mystery of selfhood

Alice, in *Alice in Wonderland*, was clearly flummoxed, 'bewitched, bothered and bewildered' when the somewhat testy caterpillar popped the question and demanded to know who she was. 'I – I hardly know Sir, just at the moment', the poor girl stammered; 'at least I knew who I *was* when I got up this morning, but I think I must have changed several times since then.'

Alice was and is not alone in her confusion. It's the story of the whole human race, both collectively and individually: most of us, most of the time, are somewhat 'flummoxed' by that same and frequently recurring question: 'Who am I?'

During his time in prison for his part in the plot against Hitler, the Lutheran Pastor Dietrich Bonhoeffer wrote a poem which he entitled, 'Who am I?' In that poem he contrasts the outward appearance he gives to others of confidence and courage, with his inner self, which is far from being the kind of person he outwardly gives the illusion of being: 'one person today and tomorrow another,' . . . 'a hypocrite before others'.

Bonhoeffer's experience in prison is replicated to a greater or lesser extent in much of the experience of our common humanity in our isolation and in the prisons of our own making.

The illusion of individualism

The hypothesis of the Bible, in Old and New Testaments alike, persistently traces the crisis of our human identity retrospectively through our ancestral 'family tree' to Adam and Eve when fundamental mistaken choices were originally made. Those wrong choices, rooted as they are in our collective make-up or collective psyche, as Jung would have said (whether genetic, psychological, sociological or whatever) have thrown us, as a race, off course in all directions ever since. Although our own age would reassert a militant individualism, the Bible prefers to speak in terms of the solidarity of the human race – as John Donne asserts in the title of his well-known poem: 'No Man is an Island'.

Jung, like John Donne long before him, saw below the surface and veneer of human behaviour, plumbing the depths of what he termed our 'collective human psyche' which conditions our behaviour in more ways than we might care to imagine. Such a contrary view of the human condition radically challenges the prevailing and much-trumpeted 'private morality' of our own day. Only perhaps with issues arising from our abuse of our planet and our concerns for the environment do we see a return to some kind of understanding of the solidarity of the human race with its accompanying, corporate responsibilities. There is a strong appeal to collective responsibility highlighted by a new appreciation that what I do in my backyard will have a roll-on effect environmentally, not only today but possibly for the next generation, and even, as the Bible puts it, 'to the third and fourth generation'.

This whole question of human identity is further compounded as a result of globalization and technological communication. Collectivism reduces my self-image to puny proportions as I become increasingly aware of a massively inhabited but apparently insignificant little planet earth, like a grain of sand on the 'seashore', amidst countless other galaxies beyond even our most advanced telescopic vision. Add to that, the time-scale of evolving life on Earth and we could be forgiven for abandoning any quest for meaningful identity, not only for ourselves as individuals, but also for the human race in general.

> Identity abhors a vacuum. We feel the need to know who we are, of which story we are a part, to which group we belong . . . In the great encounter at the burning bush, Moses' second question to God was, 'Who are you?' His first was, 'Who am I?' To know the answer to that question seems for most people to be singularly important. Indeed, for some sociologists, this has become the master-question of modernity.[2]

There are several reactions in the modern world to that 'master-question of modernity'. The assertive and aggressive rise in individualism is one such reaction. Taken to its logical conclusion, individualism strips us of any responsibility, both for society in general as well as for the environment. 'Doing my own thing' becomes the order of the day, occasionally with the added proviso – 'so long as it doesn't do anybody else any harm'. But we are not individuals, either by nature or by nurture, for in all shapes and sizes, from the past as well as in the present, a whole network of relationships plays a major role both in our identity as well as in our formation. Individualism, as we have now come to believe in it and to practise it, is little better than a figment of our deluded imaginations.

Function and identity

Unlike the caterpillar's encounter with Alice, in everyday practice most of us would probably avoid the question 'Who are you?', preferring the less intrusive question which is much easier to answer, as well as to ask: 'What do you do?', as though function were the best clue to identity.

God forbid, however, that our ultimate identity should be defined by what we do. Go down that road and it's not long before identity is reduced either to a number, a function or – even worse – a labelled object, boxed within a definition. Other labels have emerged that in the past would not have been seen as 'identities' at all: women, gays, lesbians, people of colour, the differently abled, senior citizens. 'Once,' writes Jonathan Sacks, 'these were *what* we were, not *who* we were.'[3]

'She's a smoker.' 'He's a homosexual.' 'She's an alcoholic.' But no! There's always so much more to a person just being a person, than what they do for a living, their particular addiction or their personal sexual orientation. First and foremost – whether a smoker, a homosexual or an alcoholic, a stamp-collector or whatever – all alike, according to the revelation of Christ, are persons made in the image of God. Each and every one of us is unique, whose true name is known to God alone. Christ would assure us that even the hairs of our heads are 'numbered', as we struggle against greater or lesser odds, to break loose from our culturally conditioned and inherited identities to become in relation to God, a unique child of God fashioned and re-fashioned into his likeness.

Our true identity is to be found at that point of intersection where what is personal and indeed as unique as my DNA inter-acts with what is corporate. In a word, that point of intersection is what we mean by relationship. Nothing needs to be lost of my unique personhood within the web of human relationships. Indeed, it is in my relationship with others, and supremely, as we shall see, in my relationship with God through Christ, that I discover both my true name and my true identity which will only be disclosed finally when I see God face to face and know as I am known.

The over-riding good news of the gospel should reassure us that 'we are God's children now; what we will be has not yet been revealed. What we do know is this: when he is revealed, we will be like him, for we will see him as he is' (1 John 3.2). So it follows that on our spiritual journey we cannot possibly know at this stage what we will look like after God's makeover is finally accomplished by the work of the Holy Spirit deep within us. Only when we are securely anchored in our true identity as children of God, in the here and now, can we walk by faith and not by sight on the spiritual journey of unending self-discovery in an increasingly intimate relationship with God.

What marvellous love the Father has extended to us! Just look at it – we're called children of God! That's who we really are. But that's also why the world doesn't recognize us or take us seriously, because it has no idea of who he is or what he's up to. But friends, that's exactly who we are: children of God. And that's only the beginning. Who knows how we'll end up! What we know is that when Christ is openly revealed, we'll see him – and in seeing him, become like him. All of us who look forward to his Coming stay ready, with the glistening purity of Jesus' life as a model for our own.[4]

So, 'Who am I?' concludes Bonhoeffer. 'Whoever I am, Thou knowest O God, I am thine.'

Notes

1   Thomas Keating, *The Human Condition: Contemplation and Transformation* (Paulist Press, 1999), p. 14.
2   Jonathan Sacks, *The Home We Build Together: Recreating Society* (Continuum, 2007), p. 79.
3   Sacks, *The Home We Build Together*, p. 76.
4   Eugene Peterson, *'Conversations': The Message Bible with its Translator* (NavPress, 2002), (Paraphrase of 1 John 3.1), p. 1935.

.

3

Identity through Relationships

Family and community

From the first day, our identity is woven inextricably into a whole web of relationships.

> One's identity is not a solitary possession, discovered through mental introversion, through disengagement from the webs of relationship, me thinking about myself. It is given by membership of one's community – the family, the clan, the tribe or the nation. One becomes a person through integration into the community, by embracing one's position and enacting one's role.[1]

Our identity begins with that formative relationship of child to mother and only emerges slowly into the realization of being a son or a daughter as the relationship with parents unfolds. Into this mix, other relationships develop, as with a brother or sister in the larger family environment, in which we deepen our sense of belonging. But the family is only the first building-block: others need to emerge as we discover an increasingly mature identity within the wider community.

Where, however, there is a breakdown in the basic family unit, sooner or later, we seek to build supplementary relationships, for better or worse, to compensate for the sense of not belonging; for all our longing, at root, is a desire to belong. In our own day the prevailing breakdown of family life has resulted in the emergence of a 'gang mentality'. This is a fascinating phenomenon. In a family where there is strong bonding, the early years of life are marked with a deep desire to fit in and to be the same as other members of the family. Only later in adolescence do we break loose with a desire to be different from the rest of the family as we assert our own unique personality.

Conversely, there are many cases today of broken family life in which the early years of conformity have never been experienced. So it is that later in adolescence the earlier and unfulfilled practice of conformity – harmless in the early years with the family – now reasserts itself, seeking a bonding of obsessive conformity in what has come to be known as the 'gang culture'. This is especially prevalent in the anonymity of our large cities: regimented dress and uniforms of various kinds, tattooing, a common lingo, and above all a strict conformity to 'go along' and to 'stick with your own kind' all help to create a militant and anti-establishment subculture.

Less insidiously, many find their identity later in life by belonging to the 'alumni' of a school or college or through membership of a sports club or a Livery Company. Although perhaps not always consciously, our desire for membership within manageable groupings is, at root, a quest for our personal identity within the wider community.

In the book of Genesis, following the creation of Adam, the Lord God declares that 'It is not good that the man should be alone' (Genesis 2.18). The revelation of God as a Trinity of Persons in community exhibiting a unity that is not uniformity, models for humanity an enriched quality of life. The single life or the life of a 'loner' is not commended in the Christian tradition. Indeed, in the Orthodox Churches of the East, priests may not be single: they must either be married or members of a religious community. Either way, the need to belong within a web of relationships is regarded as fundamental to our human nature. Independence and privacy are questionable characteristics. We only reach the full stature of our true and mature identity in the sharing of our lives with others, since no one person has all the necessary gifts to sustain life. St Catherine of Siena records in her *Dialogue* how God said to her, 'I could well have made human beings in such a way that they each had everything, but I preferred to give different gifts to different people, so that they would all need each other.'[2]

What's in a name?

At a very early stage, sometimes even before the child is born, parents name their child. Consciously or subconsciously, the name they give to their child already expresses something of their projected 'expectations' of what sort of person they would like their newborn child to be, and, when grown up, to become. Often the name given is the same as that of a parent or relative, with the expectation that the child will be something of a 'chip off the old block'. Americans tend to go even further and repeat the forename over several generations: George Bush Junior or Graham Smith III, rather in the style of kings and queens. During those early years, if the family is a viable and working unit, with the reasonable security which such a family commitment can nurture, then the personality formed in early childhood will largely conform to those cultural and family expectations, and may well be formulated in that forename or even some 'nickname' which endorses and even expresses their role and place within the family.

It is highly significant, however, when a child or an adult later in life is baptized and/or confirmed, that they should subsequently have the option of taking an additional name. This second name is intended to identify the newly baptized Christian within the wider Christian family. Similarly, when a man or woman enters the religious life of a monastery or convent, on taking their vows, they also take a further new name which identifies them and places them within their new 'family' and community.

Throughout the Bible – Old and New Testament alike – at the turning point of conversion to the new life and a new role within the community, God gives a new name. This implicitly suggests a new identity in a new and covenanted relationship with God. So Jacob, after he has wrestled with God, is named Israel. 'And the man said to Jacob, "What is your name?" And he said, "Jacob". Then the man said, "You shall no longer be called Jacob, but Israel, for you have striven with God and with humans, and have prevailed"' (Genesis 32.27–28).

In a similar way, as Jesus seeks to recast Simon in God's drama of salvation, he renames Simon as Peter, marking him out as the new man that God would re-create with a new name indicating the special role for Peter in the forthcoming community of faith. Similarly, Saul is changed to Paul, as the former persecutor of Christians is baptized and takes his place among the tribes of the New Israel of the Church.

Of particular interest for our purposes, however, is the naming of John the Baptist.

> On the eighth day they came to circumcise the child, and they were going to name him Zechariah after his father. But his mother said, 'No; he is to be called John.' They said to her, 'None of your relatives has this name.' Then they began motioning to his father to find out what name he wanted to give him. He asked for a writing-tablet and wrote, 'His name is John.' And all of them were amazed. (Luke 1.59–63)

Of course they were. Such a name implied a break with the well-established practices of their culture and their traditions. Furthermore, the different name was a powerful symbol of change and a breaking of the mould. What was to be expected now of this renamed child? God alone knows, you might say. So presumably did the angel, who had first spoken to Zechariah of God's intentions and future expectations for the child. It was all in the name and would slowly be revealed as the child grew and in God's time.

Breaking with the old

If I am to become the unique person whom God truly created me to be, then there must be a break from all the cultural conditioning and projected expectations which have moulded me and nurtured me. Adolescent rebellion is nature's intuitive method for doing this. However, more often than not, all that is achieved by that rebellion is a different conformity to an alternative and different cultural conditioning with its own expectations and limitations. All such expectations, whatever their origin, are always in danger of becoming self-fulfilling predictions of the families, communities, tribes and nations in which we were born and nurtured, with their self-styled and culturally conditioned programmes for happiness and human fulfilment. The seductive power of all advertisements, whether on television or on bill-boards, dupes us by enticing us to buy or to 'sign up' for their various products, by using this bait of a fulfilled, happy and successful life.

Parents, however loving and caring, as well as communities, however open and flexible, are still programmed with the expectations of a world dominated by illusion and fantasy, looking in the wrong direction for its fulfilment and happiness. In simple terms there has to be a break from the old order, with all its former cultural conditioning, if we are to inherit the new which God holds out to us. For it is precisely such communities – whether of family, small villages or the claims of larger social groupings and not least those with national and even denominational loyalties – which can hold us back, though frequently, of course, with the 'best of intentions'.

There is a striking incident in the New Testament when Jesus restores the sight of a blind man. The blind man was brought to Jesus by some well-intentioned villagers who significantly requested, not that Jesus should restore his sight, but simply that Jesus would 'touch' him. A careful reading of the text could assume that the villagers simply wanted Jesus to bless the man and to endorse the *status quo*, yet nothing so radical or perhaps even so disturbing as to open the eyes of the blind man so that he might regain his sight. Is this yet another example of how, as so often – even in the name of good and charitable works – we still want God to endorse the *status quo* rather than that radical transformation which God holds out to us in Christ?

Jesus 'took the blind man by the hand, and led him out of the village'. After Jesus had ministered to the man and restored his sight clearly (in this particular case, gradually rather than instantaneously), Jesus gave the directive to the healed man, 'Do not even go into the village' – back to your former environment. In order to live the new life with its totally new perspective, the re-envisioned man needed to return to his proper home. All this would seem to imply that the new life would be seriously inhibited back in the old environment, with all its limited and 'parochial' expectations projected on the blind man over so many years. The new, thoroughly 'rounded man' has literally been re-envisioned and simply would no longer fit into the claustrophobic 'square hole' of his former life. An emerging new life requires us at some point to 'flee the nest' as the saying goes, if it is to mature rather than fixate (see Mark 8.22–26).

It is in this context and against this background that we should read the astonishing words of Jesus – 'Whoever comes to me and does not hate father and mother, wife and children, brothers and sisters, yes, and even life itself, cannot be my disciple' (Luke 14.25, 26).

We often speak of the 'ties' of family life – but in a good sense, or as 'blood being thicker than water', as the saying goes. After all, the commandment 'to honour father and mother' should still hold good and not least in a society such as our own, where family breakdown is so prevalent. But wherever those family ties inhibit growth and hold us back, they need to be cut in order to release us to play our part in the larger community. For the family is intended to be the basic building block, but always in order to enable a larger building – community and society. So in the teaching of Jesus – admittedly using the teaching skills of hyperbole and exaggeration in order to arrest the attention of his hearers – he is, in effect, saying that we 'honour father and mother' best when we grow beyond them as sons and daughters, and as we become their mature friends in the wider family of the community.

So, 'blood *is* thicker than water', but Jesus, as he said to Nicodemus, has come to initiate the larger family of God, in which we are 'born again' of 'water and the Spirit'. 'Blood is thicker than water', but 'water and the Spirit' combined are far more binding than blood. There is a real sense in which the words of Jesus to the confused Nicodemus are all too painfully true: 'Unless a man is born of water and the Spirit, he cannot see the kingdom of God.' That break and final cutting of the umbilical cord is a kind of 'death' – a letting go of former attachments, as we shall see later, and all this in order to move forward to what God is doing in us and preparing for us.

So the naming at baptism and subsequent renaming through this 'birthing' of the Holy Spirit are so much more than just a 'rebranding'. The new name, the new product and a 'new creation' constitute a 'package deal' in the long process and the bumpy ride of being re-created and re-fashioned not only in the image of God, but ultimately also in his likeness.

Paul, writing to the new Christians in Rome, explicitly says, 'Do not be conformed to this world, but be transformed by the renewing of your minds' (Romans 12.2). Such an admonition implies a refusal to settle down, persistently urging the need to break the mould.

Don't become so well adjusted to your culture that you fit into it without even thinking. Instead, fix your attention on God. You'll be changed from the inside out . . . Unlike the culture around you, always dragging you down to its level of immaturity, God brings the best out of you, develops well-formed maturity in you.[3]

Yet, like the healing of the blind man, all this is not instantaneous. It certainly is a long process involving true commitment and not just a 'one-night stand', if the planting of the new seed of the new life is to take hold. The spiritual journey, for us as for Abraham the father of faith, is necessarily a journey from the known to the unknown, as God gently, patiently yet persistently, in an ever-deepening relationship of trust and love, reveals to us his true identity. At the same time, it is in that relationship that our own true identity is slowly revealed, as we move from false securities to our ultimate and true security; from illusion to reality concerning both God's identity as well as that of our own. For as the old definition of a true radical puts it: 'You can only explore the circumference and go to the edges, if you are sufficiently secure at the centre.'

On that journey of self-discovery in relation to God, we shall come to know by experience that our only true security is not in what we possess or even what we achieve. Rather, true security is rooted in God's faithfulness to bring to perfection what he has begun. Our part in that process, as we shall see later, is essentially to surrender our self-sufficiency and to take hold of the sufficiency held out to us by the all-sufficient grace of God, appropriated through prayer, both personal and corporate, and sustained both by word and sacrament.

In short, this whole quest for our identity is never discovered outside the context of relationships – divine as well as human. It is only as we come to know the distinctive 'other' in relationship that we discover our own distinctive identity. I am, because God is, and they are. When Moses encountered God in the burning bush he asked those two inter-related questions: 'Who are you?' and 'Who am I?' The two identities are inextricably bound together.

My own unique identity is discovered only in relationship – both in my relationship with God as well as with my neighbour. It follows, as St John confidently asserts, that it is simply not possible to love God whom we have not seen, if we do not love the neighbour whom we have seen (1 John 4.20). The structure of our relationships is both horizontal as well as vertical, and somewhere at that point of intersection is where I discover my own unique identity in an unfolding process of friendship and intimacy.

Jesus prayed, 'This is eternal life, that they may know you, the only true God, and Jesus Christ whom you have sent' (John 17.3). True life is essentially life in relationship: conversely life in isolation is a living death – a 'cut-flower' existence, exhibiting to all appearances the signs of life, yet without the sustenance of that inner life drawn from the sap of life itself. This knowledge of God of which Christ speaks is the knowledge born of relationship ('connaitre' in French), rather than informational knowledge ('savoir') or speculative knowledge. We read in the Old Testament that the boy Samuel 'did not yet know the LORD'; that is, that he had not, as yet, entered into a personal relationship with God, though doubtless he would already, from the teaching of Eli, have known a great deal *about* the Lord (1 Samuel 3.7). We shall return again and again in the course of the book to this distinction between these two kinds of knowledge – the former arising from speculation and information, as opposed to the self-revelation of God in Christ and the inspiration of the Holy Spirit.

It is in the fostering and deepening of our relationship with God, as we pray in and with Christ to his Father and ours through the Holy Spirit in prayer and worship, that the 'veil' is removed, revealing the true face of Jesus, and therefore the true likeness of his Father. 'Born again' and drawn ever more deeply into that greater circle of love, I shall discover my true self, and come to know, even as I am known.

Notes

1   Timothy Radcliffe, *What is the Point of Being a Christian?* (Burns & Oates, 2006), p. 135.
2   Catherine of Siena, *Dialogue* 7.
3   Eugene Peterson, *'Conversations': The Message Bible with its Translator* (NavPress, 2005), p. 1762.

4

The Face of
True Humanity

Envious comparisons

Conventional wisdom would teach us that, as the saying goes, 'comparisons are odious', and not least because they can all too often lead to that corrosive attitude of envy – that envy as portrayed in that shadowy face in the background of the painting by Lemoyne. Once we understand that each of us is created to be unique, it follows that we should not compare ourselves with any other human being – either favourably or unfavourably. We will never become who we were uniquely created to be by looking over our shoulder at others in an attitude of envy and its twin brother – covetousness.

There is a telling account in the last chapter of John's Gospel when Jesus is talking with Peter about his future:

> Jesus said to Peter, 'Very truly I tell you, when you were younger, you used to fasten your own belt and to go wherever you wished. But when you grow old, you will stretch out your hands, and someone else will fasten a belt around you and take you where you do not wish to go.' (He said this to indicate the kind of death by which he would glorify God.)

A daunting prospect indeed! Not surprisingly, Peter reacts very unfavourably, and so we read on: 'Peter turned and saw the disciple whom Jesus loved following . . . When Peter saw him, he said to Jesus, "Lord, what about him?"' (John 21.18ff).

'Yes', you might say – 'and what about your blue-eyed boy? If I must face a terrible death for your sake, Lord – why me and not him?' It turned out that John, 'the disciple whom Jesus loved', was the only one of the apostolic band who was not martyred and who lived on to a ripe old age as the much revered Bishop of Ephesus.

There is something in Peter's understandable attitude, not dissimilar to that of the faithful psalmist who is having a hard time of it while he looks with envy on others – unfaithful and wicked – who appear to be having a ball! 'I envied the proud and saw the prosperity of the wicked: for they suffer no pain, and their bodies are sleek and sound; in the misfortunes of others they have no share; they are not afflicted as others are.' And so the envious psalmist freely admits: 'When I tried to understand these things, it was too hard for me' (Psalm 73.16).

Paraphrased and reading between the lines, the reply of Jesus to Peter is quite stern and uncompromising, rebuking such envy and comparison. 'What is that to do with you? You just follow me and stop looking over your shoulder.'

There must be few people who at some point in their lives are not dissatisfied with their lot and who don't compare themselves enviously with others who appear more fortunate than themselves in their appearance or their station in life. All too often our response to such dissatisfaction and envy, born of comparisons, is to model and remodel ourselves on those who are in the limelight of stage or sport, so vividly and persuasively communicated through the media. Much of this, of course, may be comparatively harmless, except where it arises from a self-destructive insecurity. The celebrity culture so prevalent in our own day feeds on this kind of insecurity.

Reinventing ourselves

There is much talk today of reinventing ourselves. Of course at the superficial level of cosmetics and outward appearance, something of this reinvention may well be achievable, yet much of what motivates this whole fashionable enterprise is little better than a deep sense of insecurity – the desire to look younger, or slimmer, or whatever. For example, those who resort to plastic surgery, a facelift or tattoos, are often motivated by this deep sense of insecurity, and a lack of self-worth, in the misguided belief that what is superficial will be impressive and make them more acceptable and attractive to others. Yet all such attempts at self-improvement beg the question: 'What should the finished product look like?' as well as that earlier question, 'Who am I and why was I created?' For surely, if I have failed to come to terms with who I truly am, 'warts and all', and who I was created to be, then how on earth can I ever know what the so-called 'reinvented' features, let alone the more subtle attributes, should become? What should I change from the original; what will I 'dump', cut out in any literal or metaphorical plastic surgery, and what will I retain of the original product? So the recurring question whenever it comes to change and reinvention, or whatever: 'In which direction and to what end?'

On a journey of any kind it is surely the final destination which determines direction and all decision-making on the way. We are out on the road and come to a T-junction. Shall we turn right or shall we turn left? The answer to that question is totally determined by our ultimate destination. Until we have some clue of where we want to end up, the route we should take and how we will get there has little or no meaning.

Since the work of Darwin in the nineteenth century, there has been an increasing preoccupation with the question of the origins of the human race. Of course that is an important question. It is far more important, however, at this stage when the future destiny of the human race is so much more in our hands, to formulate the destination of all our evolutionary struggles. For neither travel nor change in themselves necessarily imply progress. Where are we evolving to? What sort of world do we want to leave for our grandchildren? Where is it all leading? In what sort of direction are so-called developing countries being encouraged to develop? And all this, when humankind is daily acquiring ever more wonderful skills to prolong and enrich life in so many ways. Yet, still, there is no escape from the disturbing fact that *destination defines decision-making* – all that T-junction business and at precisely the time when so many ethical and ideological decisions have to be made at so many turning points and junctions in the course of the human journey!

At the present time, it's as though humanity is on a journey to nowhere, driving on a hunch, intuition, or just pot luck or 'doing what comes naturally' and hoping for the best. Yet subconsciously as a race, there is an underlying, largely unspoken fear that some of our decisions may either in the short term or the longer term prove to be irreversible as we teeter on the very brink of being able, in hidden and anonymous laboratories, to clone and create, let alone re-create life in various forms.

Are we in danger of becoming – in the words of the Beatles' lyric of the last century – 'nowhere' people, 'living in a nowhere land', making lots of 'nowhere plans', not knowing where we're 'going to'?

Mentors, heroes and icons

So, of course, as the human story unfolds, we will always need models, heroes and icons, not in order slavishly to copy them or to seek to remodel ourselves on them, but as guides with experience of the journey. They can leave us clues along the route to where the ultimate treasure is to be found – the treasure of what it is to be truly and fully human, as unique men and women, created in the likeness of our Creator. As we continue to walk by

42

faith and not by sight and, picking up on what we said earlier about models, mentors and heroes, thankfully it would seem that God has provided us with signposts and icons as we journey on towards that final destination in which all will be revealed.

Jesus himself promised that there would be many staging posts, or resting places, generously prepared for us on the journey to our ultimate home and resting place, and all situated within the loving providence of God. Of course there is always the danger that such staging posts can become substitutes for the finishing post, with the accompanying temptation to settle for the puny 'motel' rather than pressing on to the glorious accommodation of our Father's house – the final resting place where we ultimately belong and where we will be totally accepted for who we are, rather than for anything we may have achieved. All such icons, together with those guides, mentors and heroes, whether from the past or contemporary, can help us to know where we are and who we are as we travel from all our false securities to our ultimate maturity, re-fashioned in the likeness of God.

After the Second World War, when I was only nine years old, my father had what we termed in those far-off days a 'nervous breakdown'. For over a year he was unable to work and was in deep depression. He was subjected to the crude electric-shock treatment, the best available at the time, which was given somewhat at random for those coming out of the horrors of the war. He did recover more or less after a year or so, but was never quite the same person. It was as though his personality was almost neutered by the somewhat crude and random electric-shock treatment offered at that time. So as a young boy of nine, it felt as though I no longer had the father I had once known, and from whom part of my early identity was derived.

Throughout all my growing-up years and indeed into later life, I moved from one mentor and hero to another. I became a good mimic, and indeed still am, so I'm told, to this day. I copied many of their mannerisms and identified very strongly with them – one after another. In the early days of that 'bereavement', my mentors were mostly teachers, but later priests and scholars, writers and even latterly, bishops! Nevertheless, I truly believe that my own vocation to the priesthood was communicated to me through such iconic figures. I was fascinated by the lives of the saints and especially by the saintly figure of Bishop Edward King who had been Bishop of Lincoln between 1885 and 1910 – long since dead, yet still figuring in my imagination and psyche with remarkable power and influence as only saints can do. The amazing sculpture of Bishop King in the Galilee Porch of Lincoln Cathedral, which acted as the Chapel for Lincoln School and which I attended as a boy, still features powerfully in my imagination to this day.

I'm sure many will scoff at what many schooled in psychology and behavioural studies would write off as 'transference'. Yet I still believe that such identification and 'looking up' to others can, if properly handled by all concerned, help us to 'grow up'. They are all – or can be – something of an interim arrangement to 'customize' the details of the journey. Yet all this assumes that we do not get stuck and turn icons into idols or signposts into finishing posts – mistaking those 'resting places' of which Jesus speaks for our ultimate destination. We need to take hold for a while of everything and everyone who in themselves are markers on that journey of self-discovery, yet always with a view to letting go, both on the part of the mentor, as well as the one who is being mentored. In seeking my final identity with its accompanying name, I must not seek to take up 'permanent residence' in any one of those resting places, nor slavishly replicate or seek to clone my mentors or heroes.

So in St Matthew's Gospel Jesus cautions: 'Call no one your father on earth, for you have one Father – the one in heaven. Nor are you to be called instructors, for you have one instructor, the Messiah' (Matthew 23.9). These sayings of course neither contradict the commandment about honouring father and mother, nor do they deny us the appropriate use of our earthly icons, mentors and guides. Yet Christ's words would warn us that the proper use of all these props and icons is to allow them to point beyond themselves to the greater reality of which they are, at best, only reflections and tasters, urging us on to the source of all that is God's best for us, which is always, by definition, 'beyond'.

True, real and substantial 'fatherhood' is only finally and fully realized in God our Father in heaven, from which all pale and greater or lesser projections, imitations and reflections derive their true identity and integrity. Even the best on earth at every level, C. S. Lewis maintains, is but 'the scent of a flower we have not found, the echo of a tune we have not heard, news from a country we have never yet visited'.[1]

Iconoclasm

In order to engage with all icons appropriately, we will always need something of that healthy spirit of iconoclasm to release us from the temptations to idolatry, and so allowing us to move on. Christ would urge us not to settle for anything less than the best – not even something we regard as quite good, yet ultimately not good enough. Repeatedly, it is the good and not only the bad that robs us of the best. The trouble is that we are satisfied too easily and too prematurely.

So the secret of avoiding spiritual travel-sickness is to follow the signposts to where they are pointing and to press on. As the Epistle to the Hebrews rightly reminds all travellers on the spiritual journey, 'Here we have no lasting city, but we are looking for the city that is to come' (Hebrews 13.14). In our prayer life God gives us all kinds of 'consolations' to encourage pilgrims on the road to that heavenly city, but at every turn in the road, as St Teresa reminds us in her *Autobiography* – we must 'seek the God of consolations and not the consolations of God'. The danger is always to mistake the copy for the reality, the icon for what it points to and the signpost for the finishing post. True pilgrims simply cannot afford to stand still, like those two disciples on the road to Emmaus – the road to further revelations – otherwise it will be recorded of us, as it was by Luke of them, that we also 'stood still looking sad'. It's at that point so often that the pilgrim glow begins to fade; we laugh less, becoming self-consciously introspective; over concerned with immediate trivia as we take our eyes from the horizon back to our domestic and nostalgic concerns of 'the good old days'! And all this while God has so many more inexhaustible delights that he longs to show to us and to share with us, further down the road.

George Tyrell, a Roman Catholic priest of the nineteenth century, reminds us of this with a vivid analogy about the appropriate use and place of mentors and heroes. Properly perceived, they are gifts from a gracious and loving Father, yet like everything in this world they are only provisional, helping us to move on. Like well-tailored suits of clothing, if we are to continue to grow, we must grow out of them.

George Tyrell's analogy is drawn from the evening Office of *Tenebrae* in which all the candles are slowly extinguished one by one, leaving at the end of the service only one candle still burning, and that the highest of them all at the top of the pyramid-shaped candle stand.

As at *Tenebrae*, one after another, the lights are extinguished, till one alone – and that the highest of all – is left, so it is often with the soul and her guiding stars. In our early days there are many – parents, teachers, friends, books, authorities – but, as life goes on, one by one, they fail and leave us in deepening darkness, with an increasing sense of the mystery and inexplicability of all things, till at last none but the figure of Christ stands out luminous against the prevailing night.[2]

Christ-shaped humanity

'You have one instructor, the Messiah' and he and he alone is our ultimate and lasting guide and mentor on the spiritual journey and 'the race that is set before us', constantly 'looking to Jesus the pioneer and perfecter of our faith' (Hebrews 12.2). For Christians believe that Jesus came to show us God's way of being truly human. We see in Jesus Christ a quality of life which is immensely enriched, abundant and outgoing. The fundamental motivation in God's mission to the world in the person of Jesus is summarized when Jesus said: 'I came that they might have life, and have it abundantly' (John 10.10). Christ and Christ alone signals the ultimate destination of all our decision-making on the way. He and he alone is the model for all who seek to be re-modelled. Reinvention, on our terms and according to our home-spun prescriptions, is out of the question.

For the quality of life we see exemplified in the person of Jesus contradicts many of our imagined characteristics. Jesus came to reveal the nature of true humanity, and a life worth living is certainly what is on offer, but not in the way that our western, consumerist society would recognize. The epitaph on the tomb of our western civilization might well read: 'Everything to live with and nothing to live for.' It's as though we were created to use things and love people, but that we have ended up loving things and using and abusing people. For, sadly, in the kingdoms of this world, it really is a matter of 'every man for himself': the law of the jungle and the survival of the fittest. Perhaps from a Darwinian perspective that is what has brought us to where we are. Rest assured, however, that it certainly will not get us to where we finally need to be.

In God's Kingdom and worldview, far from it being a question of 'every man for himself', it is in all essentials the very opposite. Jesus, who shows us the Way to true Life, exhibits an enriched life in which it is always 'man for others'. The principal characteristic of the new humanity revealed to us in the person of

Christ challenges us to cross over from a *self-serving* love to that unconditional *self-giving* love, as exemplified in Christ, who said of himself that he 'came not to be served but to serve, and to give his life' (Mark 10.45).

However, when Jesus said that we should be 'perfect' as our 'Father in heaven is perfect' (Matthew 5.48) he was most certainly not advocating a perfectionism or that his disciples should aim to be perfectionists. Far from it, even if it were possible. The word used here in the Greek – *teleios* – gives us our word 'teleology'. Teleology is the study of the 'end' of things – the ultimate purpose for which they exist.

As we have seen, all our attempts at change and the reinvention of self, beg that fundamental question concerning the end and purpose of everything. 'Perfect' in this sense implies that we become the real and authentic people we were created to be: to be truly and uniquely who we are, in the same way as God is truly God – 'perfect' in that sense. So the challenge is simply to live out our God-created identity, rather than our deluded and illusory identity, reflecting as it inevitably does our supposed, projected and equally deluded identity and character of God. When Moses asked God to reveal his name, he was given the inscrutable and yet realistic reply: 'I am that I am.'

So the secret on our spiritual journey – a secret, well and truly tested by true guides as opposed to those blind guides spoken of by Jesus – is to keep moving. It is only at the final finishing post that all will be revealed, beyond our wildest imaginings.

There, and only there, at the finishing post of the narrow way, which had demanded hand-luggage only, and precious little at that, a glorious highway opens up, generously broader the further we go as, like homing pigeons, we are irresistibly drawn to our true home and resting place in God's Kingdom of truth and love. There, with those masks of our immature fantasies finally removed, and the counterfeit of our various wrappings finally cast aside, the truth, as Christ promised, will finally set us free to become beyond time, all that before time we were originally created to be.

Notes

1   C. S. Lewis, *They Asked for a Paper: Papers & Addresses* (Geoffrey Bles Ltd, 1962), p. 200.
2   George Tyrell, quoted in Nicholas Sagovsky, *On God's Side* (Oxford University Press, 1990).

5

Liberating Our Desires

Attachments and addictions

St John of the Cross reminds us that even the finest thread attached to a bird will still make it impossible for the bird to exercise its freedom in flight. Until the thread is cut, the bird is earthbound and unable to be its true self – the bird in flight – that it was created to be. Similarly, there is much that ties us down, inhibiting and restricting the full expression of our true humanity, and that enriched and abundant life held out to us by Christ, who came that we might have life and have it in all its fullness. Our upbringing and the cultural conditioning of both nature and nurture – good in parts, like the curate's egg – nevertheless hold out to us all kinds of self-styled programmes for happiness, fulfilment, wealth and success, with the promise and expectation of freedom to become the person society will regard as successful and happy.

Yet in practice and in the course of time, the very opposite proves to be the case. So many of the objects and persons, aims and ambitions which we had desired and to which we had become attached frequently go into reverse and begin to take hold of us. Things which we had freely chosen as objects of our desire and for our enjoyment no longer give the pleasure, enjoyment or fulfilment that they had promised at the outset. It is precisely at this point that we find ourselves 'hooked' as we say, unable to break loose, move on and freely to attach our desires elsewhere. This occurs most frequently when we have attributed to anything or anybody an ultimate satisfaction that nothing nor anybody other than God could ever possibly fulfil. In a word, this wrong directing of our longings and desires for fulfilment is nothing short of idolatry. St Augustine spent the first 33 years of his life attaching his passionate desires and longings to all kinds of substitute 'gods', only to discover after many years that nothing and no one other than the true God could ever fulfil him and set him free from his self-imposed emotional bondage. Made by God and for God alone, he finally came to realize that our hearts are 'restless till they find their rest in God'. In the fourteenth century, Richard Rolle, in words that are as applicable today as when they were first written, wrote:

> Since the human soul is capable of receiving God alone, nothing less than God can fill it; which explains why lovers of earthly things are never satisfied. The peace known by lovers of Christ comes from their heart being fixed, in longing and in thought, in the love of God; it is a peace that sings and loves and burns and contemplates.[1]

The derivation of the word 'attachment' is from the old French word 'attache' which literally means 'nailed to'. So while at the outset of attaching our desires to this, that or the other according to our latest whim, seemingly exercising our free will, such freedom as we originally asserted turns out, after all, to be an illusion. We're stuck and literally 'nailed', no longer free to shop around at will as we originally supposed. The 'treasure' we chose as something or someone to be attached to, fails to fulfil what it appeared to promise in prospect. Furthermore, what had at the outset originally satisfied our desires, our hunger or thirst (whether literally or metaphorically), no longer 'does the trick'. Like Oliver Twist, we return to the source still hungry, demanding more, and subsequently more and more, because enough proves never to be enough. So we are hooked and literally 'nailed'. It is at this point that attachment can move on into addiction.

> I am not being flippant when I say that all of us suffer from addiction. Nor am I reducing the meaning of addiction. I mean in all truth that the psychological, neurological, and spiritual dynamics of full-fledged addiction are actively at work within every human being. The same processes that are responsible for addiction to alcohol and narcotics are also responsible for addiction to ideas, work, relationships, power, moods, fantasies, and an endless variety of other things.[2]

Detachment

Detachment, supposedly the opposite of attachment, is in the vocabulary of most religious traditions and yet it is a word widely open to being misunderstood. Repeatedly, over the years, many have misguidedly practised detachment with the implication that the spiritual life or the spiritual journey is best pursued by repressing our desires to the point of total indifference to everything and everyone around us. This is a total misunderstanding. On the contrary, detachment properly understood gives back the freedom to direct or redirect our desires at will.

Detachment should not imply the neutering of our passions in the sense of freeing us *from* desire. On the contrary, far from detachment leading to freedom *from* desire, properly understood and practised, detachment leads to a freedom *of* and *for* desire. This should never take the form of repressing our desires. Rather, we suppress any desires for lesser objects or persons so that we might be free to express more fully a greater desire for a more appropriate object or person to which we should direct our desires.

'An authentic spiritual understanding of detachment', writes Gerald May, 'devalues neither desire nor the objects of desire.' On the contrary, 'detachment uncovers our basic desire for God and sets it free. With freedom of desire comes the capacity to love, and love is the goal of the spiritual life.'[3]

Meister Eckhart goes even further in affirming the right practice of detachment, claiming that, rightly understood and practised, detachment 'enkindles the heart, awakens the spirit, stimulates our longings and shows us where God is'.[4]

In this way, detachment opens up the way to a true liberation of our desires, releasing them from the illusory and seductive promises of idolatry and actually stimulating our longings to press on further to the true goal of the only One who ultimately can satisfy and fulfil all our desires. Instead of 'losing our hearts', the liturgy of the Church from the earliest days exhorts us to 'lift up our hearts', for where our true and lasting treasure is, there are our hearts also (Matthew 6.21).

So detachment is never meant to imply a life in limbo. We 'detach' from the lesser in order that we might be free to 'attach' to the greater in what is sometimes termed 'an expulsive affection'. So the road to freedom is clearly marked on the spiritual journey but it leads in one direction only – namely to the one true God who alone can fulfil our deepest desires, while not holding us in bondage to himself. For this is the ultimate paradox: when we are most attached to God, then we are sufficiently detached from everything else, to the point where we can truly enjoy and delight in the rest of creation. Instead of being possessed by our possessions, we are free at last to be possessed by God in whose possession and service – even 'slavery' – we discover the reality of true and perfect freedom.

One of the many dangerous half-truths of the post-Enlightenment is the unquestioned assumption that we were born to be free and that freedom is naturally inherent in the human condition. Nothing could be farther from the truth. The tragedy of the so-called 'Rich Young Ruler' in the Gospels was that he had become possessed by his possessions. Despite his lifelong desire to belong, he had ended up belonging to his belongings – attached and 'nailed' to them and imprisoned by them. When

Jesus offers him the freedom of release, with the opportunity to fulfil truly his deepest desires and longings, he cannot break free and reattach himself to Jesus in whom alone true freedom could be found. It's as though Jesus were saying to the young man, 'Let go of those possessions which possess you, stick with me and I will set you free.'

It's important to take note that Jesus did not tell the young man to go home, to get rid of all his possessions and then just to live an empty life, in an empty house. Jesus gives the young man a double commandment: 'Go and sell all that you have – cut the ties.' But then and at the same time, 'As you detach your desires and yourself from those possessions, re-attach both your desires and yourself to me – follow me.' A 'detached' life is no life at all. In the parable of the unclean spirit, Jesus deliberately cautions against leaving 'the house empty, swept and put in order' – sanitized. True spirituality, like nature 'abhors a vacuum'.

Jesus said, 'So if the Son makes you free, you will be free indeed' (John 8.36) – words affirmed by Paul from experience, possibly bitter experience – when he testified to the Galatian Christians, 'For freedom Christ has set us free' (Galatians 5.1). And that challenge of Jesus to the young man is the challenge to all of us: to break loose from the bondage of false attachments, resulting in addiction as endured by the false self, and reach out, 'nailing' our colours to the cross of Christ, in whom alone we will discover liberation and freedom from the illusion and delusions of idolatry, fully expressed in true worship of the one true and living God.

Worship and self-transcendence

In real terms, addiction is in fact wrongly directed worship. 'Why was I created?' asks the Scottish Catechism. 'I was created to worship God and to enjoy him for ever.' If that statement is true, then it follows, whether churchgoers or not, or whether 'religious' or not, that we will inevitably worship something or somebody. The 'Golden Calf' syndrome is always with us in one form or another, however sophisticated we may think we are and whether we call ourselves religious or not. As the psychiatrist says to the young teenager in Peter Shaffer's play 'Equus': 'If you don't worship you'll shrink, it's as brutal as that.' Fundamentally and literally we were made for worship; that is to say, we only become truly human and discover our true self in self-transcendence: we are by nature compulsive worshippers in that sense.

There are all kinds of ways we seek to achieve that self-transcendence. What is sometimes explained as 'crowd hysteria' is largely fuelled by the need – even the craving – to escape into self-transcendence, whether at a game of football or in a crowded auditorium or in those 'magic' moments of music, ballet or opera. All orators, from Cicero to Hitler, intuitively knew the power of oratory, not least in the presence of a crowd. Crowds when they are 'moved' frequently begin to 'chant'. In all forms of worship and self-transcendence, music plays a particularly vital role, precisely because it has the power to bypass all the checks and balances of the analytical activities of the mind: 'It blew my mind', as we sometimes say.

But this self-transcendence born of worship can take more sinister forms, as in the drug culture or even in violent, sadistic sexual activity. Much of youth anger, protest and unacceptable behaviour, as in that play 'Equus', results from the inability to find appropriate means and ways to this self-transcendence. In short, whether we like it or not, worship we will, in one way or another.

The ultimate question to ask, then, is: What is the appropriate and authentic object or persons to which our worship and all our desires and longings should be directed? For the only difference between the worship of all the false gods and idols on offer in the supermarket of life, and the worship of the one true and living God, is that the worship of idols 'hooks' us and 'nails' us with a craving they can never fully satisfy, robbing us of our freedom. Just when we think we are riding the waves, we experience an undertow pulling us down, with the potential to destroy us. On the other hand, the worship of the one, true God gives back to us our freedom, as best we can bear it and exercise it.

So it is with God. As we worship him and give our hearts more and more to him, drawn and attached to him in worship and self-transcendence, so in turn we catch the family likeness of the Trinity with all the freedom of the true love and life of the Father and the Son in the love and freedom of the Spirit. For the irony in all of this is that we become what we worship: we take on something of that transcendent Other, which is why we sometimes observe that those who keep pets can begin to look a little like their pets, as well as the other way about!

In all of this we can now see why detachment should not result in the death of our desires, but rather the death of our false self, which is frequently driven to attach those desires to objects that can never possibly fulfil our deepest longings. Far deeper than our sexual desires, our dreams and passions is the deep desire and longing for God, for that self-transcendence in which we are literally 'lost in wonder, love and praise'. As we transcend the limitations of our natural self, we lose ourselves – that is to say the old, false self in ever-expanding experiences of freedom: the freedom to be our true self as God is free to be God.

Notes

1   Richard Rolle, *The Fire of Love* (Penguin Classics, 1971), Chapter 11, p. 76.
2   Gerald D. May, *Addiction and Grace: Love and Spirituality in the Healing of Addictions* (HarperCollins, 1991), p. 3.
3   May, *Addiction and Grace*, p. 15.
4   E. Colledge and B. McGinn (trans.), *Meister Eckhart* (Paulist Press, 1981), p. 294.

6

All Change

A change of direction

'Here below to live is to change', wrote Cardinal John Henry Newman in his *Essay on Development*, 'and to be perfect is to have changed often.'

In order to become who we were truly created to be ('perfect', in the teleological sense), we will need to change many times, and not just our outer clothing. Something more radical than a mere cosmetic makeover is required. Left to ourselves, of course, most of us most of the time prefer to 'stay put' with that old familiar saying to support our stance: 'The devil you know is better than the devil you don't know', or that other 'common-sense' platitude, is the saying that 'a bird in the hand is worth two in the bush'. Of course such counsel is most understandable where a totally pragmatic worldview holds good, yet such a worldview is the very opposite to that of the Kingdom of God, according to the teachings of Jesus and the practice of Abrahamic faith.

Dying to live

When I was a boy in Lincoln, there was a tanner's shop at the top of Steep Hill. Written in large, archaic lettering over the window, and under the name of the owner of the shop, were words in the form of a pun: 'The Man Who Dyed to Live'. (It's a gift of course to any preacher!) Jesus, both in his teaching and in his own lifestyle was and is supremely the 'man who died to live'. And that is precisely what Jesus meant when he repeatedly spoke of the need to 'die' in order to live the new life – the need to lose life ('life' in the sense of our old, former, false and culturally conditioned lives and selves). This is essential if we are to find and take up the new life of the true self, re-made and refashioned in both the likeness as well as the image of God.

This change of heart, like all change, involves a kind of 'dying' to the old, a letting go of the familiar and of all that we have previously known, in exchange for what is necessarily – to the extent that it is new – essentially, and as yet, unknown and unproven.

In one sense, all of us have already undergone precisely that kind of unnerving exchange at the time of our first birth, when we left the warm, familiar world of our mother's womb and entered the totally new environment of a far larger world. Our rite of passage from our mother's womb was experienced as a constriction and narrowing in order that we might emerge into the larger world – a world as yet totally unknown, cold and bewildering with its brighter light and its more invasive sounds. As we were cut loose from that which previously attached us to the old and the former world of the womb, there was a precarious hiatus before we caught our first breath, anticipating the more bracing environment of this larger, brave new world we call 'the real world'.

Paradoxically, the parallels between the process of birth and birthing are strikingly analogous to the process of death and dying. In both cases there is a sense in which birth and death are traumatic. The entry into the larger world initially requires a narrowing and restriction of the way. Furthermore, if the foetus 'chooses' in some sense to stay with the old familiar environment and the old attachment by way of the umbilical cord, then it dies. So on the anniversary of the day of our 'deliverance' into the new life, which we fondly call our birthday, perhaps we should read again the words from Deuteronomy as a text and challenge for every subsequent birthday: 'Today I have set before you life and death, blessings and curses. Choose life' (Deuteronomy 30.19). There is perhaps a sense in which we should not only respond to that challenge on the anniversary of our first birth, but daily with the dawning of each new day together with its choices.

The deliverance from the cord of attachment actualized in our first birth is more than just an analogy for our 'second birth' of which Jesus speaks to Nicodemus. For all detachments from the known to the unknown or from the old to the new, represent a kind of 'dying' and should give us a kind of reassurance that we have been this way before – a certain kind of inner familiarity with what is involved in the passage or journey from the old to the new, from life, through a kind of 'death', to the greater life which is always beyond our familiar territory and comfort zone. These many little 'deaths' should help us to see that the tomb of our ultimate death is but another 'womb' – not an end at all, least of all a dead end! The tomb does not mark an end in any sense, but rather a new beginning in the same way that the first Easter Day was not just a happy ending to a sad story, but rather the new beginning of a totally new narrative.

So the words of Jesus to Nicodemus take on a new and poignant significance: 'Very truly I tell you, no one can see the Kingdom of God, without being born from above', let alone enter it (John 3.3). The challenge to Nicodemus is for him to see the need for a second kind of birth, detaching him from the old and delivering him into the new. This would require nothing less than a 'death' to all that had made Nicodemus a leader of the Jews, as well as to all the cultural and religious conditioning that had made him the man he was, up to that point.

On another occasion Jesus explicitly points out the difficulty for the rich – or indeed for the beautiful or the intellectually brilliant – to accept this 'death' of the old, in order that the new may emerge. It is more difficult, he says (with vivid hyperbole to drive the point home) for a camel 'to go through the eye of a needle' (Matthew 19.24). (Incidentally, so powerful did that imagery of the camel and the needle prove to be, that the phrase appears in all three of the synoptic Gospels, undoubtedly remembered as the exact words from the lips of Jesus.) So Jesus urges, 'Enter through the narrow gate; for the gate is wide and the road is easy that leads to destruction, and there are many who take it' (Matthew 7.13, 14).

Similarly, C. S. Lewis in *The Lion, the Witch and the Wardrobe* relates how the passage from the back of the mythological wardrobe into the larger dimensions beyond is through a very narrow way – but a narrow way that grows larger the further you go. All this follows, as Jesus points out, that it is extremely difficult for a person cluttered and bound by whatever 'riches' of this world, to pass through the narrow way. There must be a loss and jettisoning of all the baggage of the former self – a 'narrowing of the way' – if there is to be gain on the other side. For in this transaction, the gain follows on from the loss, as in the title of Newman's first novel *Loss and Gain*. We might even say that unless we are 'born again' and 'die' in this sense many times, we end up in dead-ends and cul-de-sacs, trapped and lost in the *status quo.*

Furthermore, at the point of that kind of 'death' with its detachment from the old, experience naturally cautions us that what is new is not immediately in evidence. There is usually a sense of anticipation when, like Abraham, the founding father of all those who have chosen faith as a way of life, we necessarily proceed only by faith – that faith, as we read in the Epistle to the Hebrews, which is defined as 'the assurance of things hoped for, the conviction of things not yet seen' (Hebrews 11.1). From start to finish, as St Paul urges, 'we look not at what can be seen but at what cannot be seen; for what can be seen is temporary, but what cannot be seen is eternal' (2 Corinthians 4.18).

We should be able to take heart, however, as we travel, for there is much in the natural world with its own distinctive evidence to support the validity of this transaction of a 'death' which gives way to new life. Perennially, the seasons of the year play out before our very eyes, the drama of this exchange of death for new life – of displacement and replacement – on the branches of trees and in our gardens. As the light decreases in autumn and winter, so the sap falls and so do the leaves and flowers. With the increase of light, in only a matter of weeks and with the dawning of spring, so the apparently dead branches break open with shoots of new life and fresh foliage.

We see less visible and more hidden evidence for this same process not only in the seasons of the year, but also in something as glorious and mysterious as the change and transformation from that 'testy' caterpillar who challenged Alice in Wonderland, into a colourfully winged butterfly. During the caterpillar stage, the caterpillar sheds several skins – four or five or even as many as nine. By the shedding of these skins (called 'instars') the caterpillar grows in preparation to pass from the life of a caterpillar into the form of 'death', taking the form of a chrysalis. The chrysalis, easily mistaken for a dead twig off a tree, gives no outward appearance of life or of change and transformation from the two-dimensional old self in its old form, to the three-dimensional and infinitely more beautiful and attractive new embodiment of a butterfly. Only by the shedding of those former skins, appropriate for its life as a caterpillar, can the creature be 'born again' in the form of a butterfly, with its new body – a quasi-resurrection body – no longer earthbound, but rather equipped for flight.

It would seem that even nature itself testifies to this kind of faith and trust with its visible and tangible encouragement to let go of the old, casting off the outer skin of our old self so that we might be free to reach forward to the new; to detach in order to re-attach, even though this inevitably involves a kind of apparent and somewhat illusory kind of death and dying.

At the very heart of life is the challenge of sacrifice; of dying to our present position in order to move to a higher level of life. This can only happen by letting go of the false self. Suffering and death are not enemies, but doors leading to new levels of knowledge and love. Unless we are willing to sacrifice what we have now, we cannot grow. We grow by dying and rising again; by dying to where we are now and being reborn at a new level.[1]

So St Paul says, 'For while we live, we are always being given up to death for Jesus' sake, so that the life of Jesus may be made visible in our mortal flesh' (2 Corinthians 4.11).

For those who rely on the intellect and on analytical reasoning – as Nicodemus in his early life clearly did – all this business of detachment and attachment, of dying and being reborn, is extremely hard to take in, let alone to follow as a way of life. Of course we prefer to write books about it, to preach and talk about it; but the ultimate challenge is to walk the talk and to live as we pray or as we aspire to pray. True prayer is not so much a specific activity but much more a whole way of life and of a new way of seeing the whole of life. The old adage should be seen to work both ways: 'In the midst of life we are in death' as the popular saying goes. But the reverse is equally true, when properly understood: 'In the midst of death we are in life' – that new life that is only liberated through the death of the old. Most of us have to learn this the hard way – out on the road. It doesn't come by way of armchair discussion groups or philosophical wrangling.

Take, for example, those Greeks who came to Jesus for some kind of theological or philosophical discussion, perhaps seeking information about that Kingdom of God which people at the time were beginning to talk about. Clearly Jesus, however, was not willing to go down that road or to offer new information in reply to their questioning. It would seem that Jesus is not so much concerned to communicate abstract information or to promote an abstract 'Christianity', stored in the mind alongside other ideologies. The prime concern of Jesus was and always is to search the hearts of all seekers and enquirers to see whether they are ready to receive not so much information, but costly transformation; the kind of transformation that only comes through the death of the old, and the willingness to open hearts and minds to receive the new. Furthermore, that transformation is only made possible if we are ready to leave behind the 'old self' with all its baggage, as the sons of Zebedee did when they left their father behind to get on with the fishing, so that they could undertake a very different kind of fishing by following Jesus, the Way to true Life, all the way as disciples on the spiritual journey. Were those Greeks ready for that upheaval? Are we?

So the only retort Jesus has for those who seek theology, philosophy or the study of God apart from a relationship with God through prayer, liturgy and scripture, is summed up in his reply to those enquiring Greeks. 'Very truly I tell you, unless a grain of wheat falls into the earth and dies, it remains just a single grain; but if it dies it bears much fruit. Those who love their life lose it, and those who hate their life in this world will keep it for eternal life' (John 12.24f).

So St Paul brings all this right into the here-and-now when he says, 'You have died' – in the sense of the old self – and your true, new life is not yet apparent because it is 'hidden with Christ in God. When Christ who is your life is revealed, then you also will be revealed with him in glory' (Colossians 3.3–4). Then at last we will outwardly look like what we are and be what we appear to be. No more of that business of keeping up appearances. As for cosmetics – well, clearly they will be redundant, left behind together with the grave clothes 'apart by themselves' (John 20.7).

Death and resurrection in the Church

All that is said above as applying to Christian disciples individually in the course of their unfolding spiritual journey also applies in every detail to the corporate life of the Church. To the extent that the Church is necessarily 'clothed' in any generation in the cultural 'skins' of the society that it is there to serve, it is necessarily an institution. The principle of the continuing incarnation demands that in every generation the Word is enfleshed. Yet beneath the outward form of an institution, and to the eyes of faith, the Church exists on earth as a sign, pointing to its ultimate and abiding identity as the Body of Christ. As such, the Church will need to undergo, as each generation passes, a shedding of its cultural 'skins' not dissimilar to the way in which the caterpillar is re-formed through a kind of 'death' into the fuller life of a butterfly.

> The mistake of ecclesiasticism through the ages has been to believe in the Church as a kind of thing-in-itself. The apostles never regarded the Church as a thing-in-itself. Their faith was in God, who had raised Jesus from the dead, and they knew the power of His Resurrection to be at work in them and in their fellow-believers despite the unworthiness of them all. That is always the true nature of belief in the Church. It is a laying-hold of the power of the Resurrection.[2]

Throughout history, many have called frequently for the 'renewal of the Church' yet without accepting the need for 'death' to precede true resurrection, corporately as well as individually. Contemplative living is a challenge to both individual disciples as well as to the Church at large, for the cult of individualism has no place in the life of the Body of Christ.

> Some people construct a Christianity which consists entirely of a personal relationship to Jesus Christ and has virtually

nothing to do with the church. Others make a grudging concession to the need for church membership, but add that they have given up the ecclesiastical institution as hopeless. Every church in every place at every time is in need of reform and renewal. But we need to beware lest we despise the church of God and are blind to its work in history.[3]

So it follows that the Church will only reveal its true identity to the extent that it is renewed everywhere and at all times as it replicates mystically the dying and rising of Christ, whose Body on earth it represents and continually re-presents. Therefore the outward forms or 'skins' of the institutional Church must be shed with each passing generation, giving the outward appearance of a kind of death. Only in this way, as the Church corporately is re-centred again in Christ, can it be raised to new life. Otherwise, if we seek to preserve the outward forms and the *status quo*, both form and substance alike will die together.

Contemplative prayer and contemplative living are essential at the heart of the Church, corporately as well as at a congregational level. Often renewal has been seen as a form of sectarianism and the reassertion of individualism. This will always occur when the Church corporately has not taken on board the challenge of the contemplative gospel.

> Without this contemplative orientation we are building churches not to praise him but to establish more firmly the social structures, values and benefits that we presently enjoy. Without this contemplative basis to our preaching, our apostolate is no apostolate at all, but merely proselytizing to insure universal conformity with our own natural way of life.[4]

In all of this, there is clearly an urgent need to recall both the Church corporately as well as disciples individually, to our true identity as members of the Body of Christ, experienced and actualized in the dying and rising of Jesus both in history as well as mystically throughout history.

Notes

1   Thomas Keating, *The Heart of the World: An Introduction to Contemplative Christianity* (Crossroad Publishing, 1981), p. 21.
2   Michael Ramsey with Cardinal Suenens, *The Future of the Christian Church* (Morehouse-Barlow Co., 1970), p. 38.
3   John Stott, *Ephesians: Building a Community in Christ* (InterVarsity Press, 1998), p. 30.
4   Thomas Merton, *The Climate of Monastic Prayer* (Irish University Press, 1969), p. 154.

7

Information, Inspiration and Transformation

Information

From time to time, on any journey, on arriving at our destination we have the experience of feeling – but only in retrospect – that all roads lead inevitably to our destination. If, however, we were to follow such an inclination during the course of the journey, the whole undertaking would most likely end in disaster. While we are travelling and navigating, all information along the way is invaluable and indispensable: only a fool would ignore the road signs and the signposts, let alone seek to dispense with road maps, even compass bearings and perhaps even more the odd piece of advice, born from experience and offered by fellow travellers who have previously taken the same or a similar journey.

So it is with the spiritual journey. Theology, tradition, church doctrine and the experience of the saints and those who are further down the road, can all offer useful information concerning direction, correction and choice of routes. In themselves, however, as travellers know only too well, it is one thing to know the way and something quite different to set out and 'to walk the talk', as the saying goes. The maps and signposts are only helpful to those who are willing to get out on the road and to pursue their destination. For the Christian pilgrim on the spiritual journey, the destination is self-evident from the outset: the new Jerusalem, the Kingdom of Heaven and the vision of God. The danger, throughout the whole journey, as we have pointed out earlier, is to mistake any one of the signposts for the finishing post, the means for the end, the illusion for the reality.

Of course we need our theologians, but, may I suggest, theologians with a difference. In an age of information-overdrive and not least since the Enlightenment in the west, the theologian speaks primarily from within the environment of the library and the lecture room, or from the pages of the written word in the environment of academia. His or her information is imparted and communicated in and through books about God. Similarly with the training of the clergy. For many of our clergy, trained in the culture of theological academia, there is the real danger that the end product of Christian or ministerial formation is a brain full of Christianity!

Compare and contrast this with what the early Church, or the Orthodox Churches of the East would mean by the word 'theologian' or indeed by 'theology' itself. 'The theologian', said Anthony Bloom, 'is not somebody who knows about God, even less someone who knows what others have written about God. The theologian is someone who knows God.' That 'knowledge', as we have previously seen, is not merely knowledge *about* God, but rather knowledge in the sense of being in a *relationship* with God. In other words, the theologian is defined in the Orthodox Churches as being the one 'who prays right'.

Similarly, the understanding of the Eastern Orthodox Churches when they speak of 'orthodoxy'. In the west we speak of orthodoxy more in the sense of constituting right belief – ticking all the right boxes in the ecumenical creeds of the Church. Not so in the Eastern tradition where orthodox means what it says in Greek – 'right praise' or 'true worship'. So the theologian in that sense pursues his or her craft more in the context of the liturgy than the library and more in the context of prayer and worship (corporate as well as personal) than in the lecture room. *Lex orandi: lex credendi* – right belief and right prayer are two sides of the same coin.

Wherever this is the case, the end product is information with a difference: information, born of inspiration, leading to formation and transformation. There is a crying need in all the churches today for both a renewal of theology in this sense, together with a theology of renewal, both alike arising from a Church rooted in contemplative prayer and contemplative living, resulting from the double grip of both word and sacrament.

So of course we need our theologians in the same way that we need guides when we are travelling, climbing or exploring: spiritual guides, who know the way from experience and as experienced navigators – holy men and women of prayer, who will not only quote from what others have said about the royal highway to the Kingdom, but rather those who will speak from their experience with that authority that comes only from those who 'walk the talk'. It was said of Jesus that he spoke as one 'having authority' and not as the scribes and Pharisees who relied upon the right quotations and word-for-word references from the law.

There is the kind of information that rightly informs the mind, and that has its place: we should never seek to bypass the mind but rather to go beyond it or rather more deeply within our cognitive awareness. Information arrested in the mind, solely as information, is ultimately rendered sterile and does not lead further to that 'warming of the heart' and the firing of the will, expressed in daily living. Such is true discipleship, quietly and confidently following Christ who is the Way and who has gone ahead to open up the way to the Father. It is Christ who fulfils God's promise, when he said to the Israelites of old that they should 'trust' in the 'LORD your God who goes before you on the way . . . in fire by night, and in the cloud by day, to show you the route you should take' (Deuteronomy 1.32f.). The same promise holds good for us on our spiritual journey. For the spiritual journey, properly understood, is the longest journey in the world, leading from mind to heart and from heart to the will where it is ultimately tested and vindicated in the everyday world of life and action.

A change of heart

The Word of God, speaking his living word *through* the written words of scripture, informs the mind, warms the heart and fires the will in this long process of spiritual formation and transformation. We need to know from the outset, however, that right information and even good education, in themselves, will not do the trick and lead to a change of heart and outlook, let alone the re-direction of our lives to which Christ calls us – in a word, repentance.

I always remember staring across the tax-free shop in Heathrow Airport where large packs of cigarettes were prominently displayed. In bold letters, clearly visible from across the shopping area on those same packs, and in large and bold letters, were the words: 'Smoking Kills'. Yet large numbers of people were still queuing at the check-out, only feet away from the large warning sign to purchase the apparently 'deadly articles'! Clearly, experience would tell us that neither information nor education by themselves necessarily lead to transformation or to a change in the direction of our lives. For repentance understood as re-direction or even the much-maligned U-turn is one of the most positive and creative words in the human vocabulary.

Repentance, however, should have little or nothing to do with guilt, for guilt is so often little more than wounded pride. St Paul contrasts two very different kinds of repentance. He tells the Corinthian Christians: 'Godly grief produces a repentance that leads to salvation and brings no regret, but worldly grief produces death' (2 Corinthians 7.10). Repentance – or '*metanoia*' in Greek – literally translated means a 'change of mind', frequently expressed as having second thoughts. The wicked Fagan in the musical *Oliver Twist* sings, 'I'm reviewing the situation . . . I think I'll stop and think it out again.' That's the kind of repentance God is looking for as we pursue our spiritual journey. So in the Epistle to the Hebrews, in the account of Esau selling his blessing and birthright we read, 'Later, when Esau desired to inherit the blessing, he was rejected, for he found no chance to repent.' Of course Esau was sorry but there was no chance for him to repent, that is to say, for him to 'change his mind' (Hebrews 12.17). Not so in our dealings with God! It is never too late to 'change our minds', our hearts and our whole outlook, to turn around and go in a new direction – even possibly in the opposite direction.

True repentance involves a radical reappraisal of all our former priorities; a reappraisal of our aims and objectives as well as a willingness to see ourselves, others and the world around us from a totally new perspective, and in contradiction to all that has gone before. The great work of Galileo revolutionized the way we view the universe, with neither ourselves nor planet Earth at the centre. 'Seeing the universe from the *I* perspective is to see it inside out or upside down or not at all.'[1]

Personal repentance involves a similar reorientation of our viewpoint, resulting in a necessary displacement of self from the centre by the replacement of God at the centre of everything. Many times *en route* we will need to pray, 'Create in me a clean heart O God, and put a new and right spirit within me' (Psalm 51.10).

Information and inspiration

As we saw previously in the distinction which the French language makes between different kinds of knowledge, coming to know God in the biblical sense is so very much more than simply knowing *about* God. So when Paul writes: 'I want to know Christ and the power of his resurrection' (Philippians 3.10), he is not referring to reading more books with information about Christ, but rather to a fresh personal knowledge of Christ in a deep, personal and intimate relationship – education in the sense of formation and transformation.

So the place of true education in this whole process is somewhat more elusive, for there is a sense in which you cannot tell anybody anything that will make a real difference in their lives unless in some sense they already know it inwardly and almost intuitively with a knowledge that doesn't connect and resonate with something already deep within them. True education 'draws out' ('*educo*') and makes explicit that which formerly had been only implicit. Such was the reason why Jesus refused to give theological soundbites ('pearls before swine') about God and his Kingdom. Rather, he preferred to teach in parables. Otherwise, as Jesus implied, his hearers would have got the 'wrong end of the stick', as we say, and would go away thinking they understood Christianity! We make knowledge our own, or, as the saying goes, 'the penny drops' when a word from *without* resonates with a word that is deeply held *within* and which in the process is drawn out and articulated – 'en-fleshed' and 'made our own'. Such was the experience of John Wesley when he heard a passage being read from the Epistle to the Romans at a prayer meeting in Aldersgate. On that occasion Wesley recorded in his diary that he 'felt that strange warming of the heart'.

All this is essentially the work of the Holy Spirit, when information and inspiration work together to bring about re-formation and transformation. So St Paul, differentiating between these two different kinds of knowledge, writes to the Corinthians:

But as it is written, 'What no eye has seen, nor ear heard, nor the human heart conceived, what God has prepared for those who love him' – these things God has revealed to us through the Spirit; for the Spirit searches everything, even the depths of God. For what human being knows what is truly human except the human spirit that is within? So also no one comprehends what is truly God's except the Spirit of God. Now we have received not the spirit of the world, but the Spirit that is from God, so that we may understand the gifts bestowed on us by God. And we speak these things in words not taught by human wisdom but taught by the Spirit, interpreting spiritual things to those who are spiritual. (1 Corinthians 2.9ff)

Such and similar experiences are given to many Christians as they open their hearts in prayer to the transforming power of God – the divine therapist, as Father Thomas Keating speaks of the re-directing of the Holy Spirit. The scriptures – Old and New Testaments alike – speak of this change of heart as information and education leading us on through true repentance and re-direction, to re-formation and transformation of life.

Such prayer essentially involves the opening of our hearts to that within us which is deeper than the comprehension of the mind or the awareness of the senses; that is to say the subconscious, which motivates our actions more than we might care to acknowledge. It is easier to open up in this way when we are on holiday, or even in sleep, when the conscious is not drowning out all that is going on in the subconscious. Sometimes, in over-busy lives, it's only in sleep or in our dreams that God has an opportunity to get a word in edgeways. That is perhaps one of the reasons why many people tend to dream more often while on vacation.

In any event, the opening of our hearts (our inner selves) to the breathing in or inspiration of the Holy Spirit to redirect and resonate with our own unique and inner spirit of which Paul speaks is at the heart of the practice of what we call Centering Prayer. In the Book of Common Prayer, the so-called 'Collect for Purity' spells this out in words that are most appropriate at the outset of worship or even our personal prayer times. 'Almighty God, to whom all hearts are open, all desires known, and from whom no secrets are hidden: Cleanse the thoughts of our hearts by the inspiration of your Holy Spirit, that we may perfectly love you and worthily magnify your holy Name; through Christ our Lord.'

A new heart and a right spirit

Ezekiel of old had spoken of God as replacing 'a heart of stone' with 'a heart of flesh'.

> I will give them one heart, and put a new spirit within them; I will remove the heart of stone from their flesh and give them a heart of flesh, so that they may follow my statutes and keep my ordinances and obey them. (Ezekiel 11.19)

In Hebrew it is made perfectly clear that only God can create a new heart. All our strivings for self-improvement are of little avail: a new heart is exclusively the work of God who alone can re-create. In the Hebrew Bible, the verb '*bara*', 'to create', is used only and exclusively of God as the Creator. Nobody else and nothing less can bring about this new creation.

The old heart is only broken in order that it is enabled to open up to the new. The psalmist takes up this theme of a new heart: 'The sacrifice acceptable to God is a broken spirit; a broken and contrite heart, O God, you will not despise' (Psalm 51.17). Our part in all of this is to consent and to allow God the space and time to work in us that which is truly pleasing in his sight. When our spirit yields in prayer to the ongoing and renewing power and work of the Holy Spirit, this process of recreation and transformation can continue unselfconsciously in our innermost selves, until God has finally perfected what he has begun.

The brokenness of which the psalmist speaks is, however, a prerequisite of this transformation from the old to the new, from the illusory and false self to the real and true self. It may take many forms.

> True worship and new living require a yielding of self to begin again on God's terms. But the brokenness may not be a psycho-

logical dismantling. It may as well be an economic unburdening, a political risking, a stepping away from whatever form of power we have used by which to secure ourselves.[2]

St Paul develops this whole theme of the new creation when he says: 'If anyone is in Christ, he is a new creation. The old has gone away.' It is questionable, however, whether in practice this transformation from the old to the new is quite so instantaneous as Paul's words might imply. St Cyprian of Carthage freely admits when writing to the Donatists that he struggled with some problems and hangovers from his former life – 'addiction to sumptuous feasts . . . and costly attire'.

> I was disposed to acquiesce in my clinging vices, and . . . I despaired of better things . . . But . . . by the help of the waters of new birth, the stain of former years was washed away and a light from above, serene and pure was infused into my reconciled heart . . . the agency of the Holy Spirit breathed . . . a second birth, restoring me to a new man; then in a wondrous manner, what had seemed difficult began to suggest a means of accomplishment; what I thought impossible to achieve.[3]

In what sense, then, do we speak of this renewing of the heart and mind and will? Is it instantaneous, and in what sense does the 'new' replace 'the old'? Is the 'old' totally obliterated to be replaced by the 'new creation'?

The analogy of Jesus concerning new wine and new wineskins is recorded in all three of the synoptic Gospels – Matthew, Mark and Luke – and was clearly a memorable saying of Jesus. But a careful scrutiny of the Greek text can help us to unravel the true meaning of 'renewal', whether in our personal lives or indeed in the life of the whole creation. Jesus uses two different words for 'new' in respect of the wine and the wineskins. For the 'new wine', the word used is '*neos*' meaning 'new' but more in the sense of the 'latest' in contrast to the 'old'. But for the wine-skins, the word used in Greek is '*kainos*', which should better be translated as 'new' in the sense of being 'fresh' or 're-newed', indicating quality rather than chronology. So 'new wine' will require 'refreshed' or 'refurbished' or 'renewed' or even recondi-tioned wineskins.

In a similar way, when Christ speaks of the old law he refuses to rubbish it or throw it away by replacing it with something totally new and unconnected with the old. So Christ speaks of 'fulfilling' the old by the 'new', transforming it into the more generous dimensions of grace. There is no intention to replace totally Plan A with a second, unrelated Plan B. Christ is at pains to make clear that the renewal of the old is God's way of bringing it to perfection – that is to say, to its true end for which it was first instituted.

And again in the case of the 'new man' referred to in the Epistle to the Ephesians (2.15), the word used is not *neos* but *kainos*, indicating no total break with the old self, but rather indicating renewal in the sense of transformation and renova-tion. In good quality renovation of distressed antique furniture, the stains and markings over the years are not totally removed. Rather, they are retained, and, after being worked on, actually blend in with the new in such a way as to retain the integrity of the whole piece.

The renewal of our hearts and lives by the outpouring of the Holy Spirit at times is necessarily painful and requires a willing-ness to accept our brokenness as part of the process of being put together again.

> To summarize, the broken-hearted person is pleasing to God not simply because he or she lacks arrogance and is humble, but above all because this experience leads one to trust no longer in one's own resources but in God's mercy and stead-fast love, the God who is the creator of a new heart. So through a broken heart, God enters.[4]

It is that resulting 'self-emptying' and openness to God's healing love, received in prayer, that constitutes the fundamental elements in this process of transformation from the old to the new. As Oscar Wilde puts it, in words born from bitter experience, in his 'Ballad of Reading Gaol': 'How else except through broken heart, may Lord Christ enter in?'

Throughout this whole process, we need to know that what is shattered is not lost because the old – albeit transferred from the debit column to the credit column – is in the new. Charles Williams speaks of this process of transference in this way: 'The old man in the old way; the new man in the old way; the new man in the new way.' Life in this world is likely to be mostly spent in that transitional period of the new man, still lingering from time to time in the old ways of weakness. We need to know that God can hold us in this tension within his unconditional and infinite love for us; that he truly knows us as we are – 'warts and all' – while at the same time holding us in his heart as he originally imagined and created us to become. Our part in this whole process of renewal and transformation is simply to go on trusting, like St Paul, that God's 'grace is sufficient' for us, and that his strength is 'made perfect in our weakness' (2 Corinthians 12.9).

God works much more freely through human weakness when it is held open to Him in faith and love than through supposed strengths operating by the wisdom of this world. His life was wholly set on the creative and saving power of God; and he taught, as he had experienced it, that the root problem for humankind is an un-readiness to receive, to stand in, and be transfigured by the power of God's glory which descends to us in Christ crucified. This would require of us that we should enter into our baptismal dying, being crucified with Christ and thereby bringing the old mode of human nature to an end, thus beginning the new mode of life given in the Risen Christ.[5]

So of course on the spiritual journey there must always be a note of realism which counters any temptation to spiritualizing either our strengths or our weaknesses. There is an inevitable overlapping of the new with the old ('sin that clings so closely') when from time to time we skid and even end up in the ditch where, I suspect, we will be surprised to find no small number of highly esteemed other travellers along with us in the same ditch! But it is at such times that we experience the unconditional and unlimited love and forgiveness of God to restore us and remake us. So, as the epistle to the Hebrews advises, we must pursue our journey 'with patience' and not be too concerned with ourselves, but rather constantly 'looking to Jesus, the Pioneer and Perfecter of our faith'.

Our times of break*down* out on the road are God's opportunity to break *through* so that such moments are not occasions for despair or undue despondency. Rather, we should return patiently and constantly to the Lord, trusting in his all-empowering grace to pick up the pieces and to continue the wondrous reordering of our lives, according to the pattern of his design and not of our own efforts for the reinvention of ourselves, however worthy.

Notes

1   Thomas Keating, *Who is God?* (Text from an audiotape transcribed by S. Stephanie Iachetta at a meeting entitled 'Contemplative Prayer in the Twenty-first Century', 30 September 2000).
2   Walter Brueggemann, *The Message of the Psalms: A Theological Commentary* (Augsburg Publishing House, 1984), p. 101.
3   Cyprian, *Ad Donatum 4*.
4   Donna Orsuto, *Holiness* (Continuum, 2006), p. 25.
5   Gilbert Shaw, *Increase of Prayer* (S.L.G. Press, Fairacres, Oxford, 1971), Introduction.

8

The Christian Foundations for an Interior Life in the Spirit

Prayer beyond the beginnings

At some point on our spiritual journey, there comes a time when we finally realize that all our attempts to formulate our understanding and knowledge of God will always elude us: he is always one step ahead of us. At the same time, however, we have an ever-deepening need to know God and to respond to his eternal and deep desire to draw close to us. It may be that we have been faithful churchgoers for most of our lives; even that we have sought to practise a disciplined 'spiritual' life – studying our faith, reading the Bible, saying our prayers and regularly attending corporate worship. Yet suddenly, or perhaps over the course of time, we feel that we have reached a dead end, and that discipleship is little more than church attendance and striving to live a good and responsible life in service and kindness to others. Such knowledge as we have of God is that kind of 'secondhand knowledge' derived from doctrine, sermons and various study courses or even retreats we have attended. 'Having faith', or, contrariwise, 'losing faith' has become largely a matter of believing in a body of knowledge *about* God, and that the clauses of the creedal statements about God are true or not true, as the case may be.

As for prayer, it is so easy to reduce both our understanding of prayer, as well as our practice of prayer, either to reciting prayers – 'saying our prayers', as we say – or to a monologue in which we do all the talking and God is supposed to do all the listening. Even if we had been taught the practice of meditation based on scriptural study, we regard it primarily as something that *we* do – *our* activity of analyzing the gospel and making applications of what we have read to our own life situation, together with resolutions as to how we should serve Christ better.

Of course all this is most important, and nothing written here should suggest that any of the above practices should be jettisoned as part of the curriculum in the 'school' of Christian discipleship. Nevertheless, we come to a point, sooner or later, when we realize that there is so much more further along the road to what is involved in being a Christian disciple and a follower of the Way – and, indeed, as in any maturing relationship. For implanted within all of us there is a deep desire and longing – a hunger and a thirst – to know God intimately. Our longing is to experience, at a level far deeper than the intellect or our senses, what can only be called (to use the vocabulary of Christ himself), a deep 'friendship' with Christ, who in turn draws us to his Father and ours. 'I do not call you servants any longer,' says Jesus, in the intimacy of the Upper Room, 'because the servant does not know what the master is doing; but I have called you friends, because I have made known to you everything that I have heard from my Father' (John 15.15).

Part of the problem is derived from our approach to knowledge which is seen, especially in the west and particularly since the Enlightenment, as mainly an analytical exercise of the brain and the accumulation of information – the paralysis of analysis. Such knowledge is useful and indeed essential in quantifying and assessing the material world, but then again only in so far as the particular material being analysed is abstract, static and accessible to one or other of our senses. When it comes to the more elusive interaction of human relationships, often the mind positively gets in the way of a personal knowledge of another person. In such situations we often find ourselves saying, 'I know a lot about him, but I can never understand him.'

Imminence and transcendence

If this is true of our knowledge about those we can see and touch and hear when they speak, how much more true it must necessarily be in our relationship with God, whom no one has seen and, according to scripture, lived to tell the tale.

> Yet in our relationship with God we need to hold together these two biblical emphases: that God cannot be seen, and yet a relationship of knowledge and intimacy is possible. God is at the same time both unapproachable and close, beyond our vision and within our hearts.[1]

It's as though God has a double hold on us: from within us as well as beyond us. For he is both imminent, closer than our next breath and yet at the same time and in the same breath, transcendent. Our failure to comprehend this is also our failure to recognize that infinity is not just lots and lots of the finite. Rather, infinity is something of another order all together, so that knowledge as an exercise of the brain, with its limited finite abilities, can never hope to comprehend that which by definition is infinite, 'beyond' and of another order altogether. By definition this other kind of knowledge, which does not rely so heavily on classified information, can be experienced only as part of a relationship in which mysterious truth is communicated through love and through the heart – the seat of all our desiring. Such communication is not given in abstract formulae, or pocketbook truths and aphorisms, but it can only be 'received' as a gift freely given by the One who is himself the Truth and can only be reciprocally and thankfully received by the beloved.

Now, of course all that is suggested here is essentially counter-cultural.

> The passivity into which the Lord eventually leads us in prayer is so contrary to our natures, and the world into which we enter is so 'upside down', that it seems the same lesson needs to be learned a thousand times over before it becomes truly our own.[2]

As we grow in times of such prayer, the words of John the Baptist become increasingly applicable to us: 'Christ must increase, but I must decrease' (John 3.30). The old ego must die, if the new ego, recreated in the likeness as well as the image of God, is to live and bear fruit. This is a recurring theme to which Jesus returns frequently in his teaching about the new life: 'Unless a grain of wheat falls into the earth and dies, it remains just a single grain; but if it dies it bears much fruit' (John 12.24).

There is always a danger that the good intentions of our discipleship, and not least even of our prayers, will be perceived simply as 'topping up' the self with a touch of God, like icing on a cake, to add to the flavouring and for presentation purposes! We need to recognize that the forced and self-conscious attempts at kindness and good works, even in the name of Christ, are often resourced from an inflated ego. If this can be true of individual Christians, how much more is there the danger of a projected 'triumphalism' on the part of the institutional Church, and especially in the case of 'successful' and large churches.

The knowledge of the heart

So if we are to grow in our relationship with God through prayer, we need at some point to review our whole approach to life, to God, and to others, expressed in what we fondly like to call 'our prayers'. The centre of awareness needs to move from the head to the heart – from the seat of thoughts and images to the seat of our desires – in the practice of what we sometimes call 'Centering Prayer'.

It was St Bonaventure and the Franciscans who emphasized this 'warming of the heart and the firing of the will' in contrast with the emphasis of the Dominican friars and the scholastics, who tended to emphasize the enlightening of the mind and the acquiring of the kind of knowledge of God that is refined through the intellect. The difference and tension between the Franciscan tradition and that exemplified by the Dominicans in this respect is a continuing tension, not only in the Church at large, but within all those who would seek a true knowledge and experience of God. It was Pascal, the great philosopher, who, on balance, emphasized what he called the 'knowledge of the heart', for it's as though knowledge needs to be bonded afresh with love, while at the same time the intellect needs to be re-centred and directed to the heart. The wise fox, in Antoine de Saint-Exupery's 'Little Prince', puts it like this: 'Here is my secret. It is very simple. It is only with one's heart that one can see clearly. What is essential is invisible to the eye.'[3]

So the knowledge we are seeking in such prayer is not and never can be the kind of knowledge derived from 'secondhand' information, but only the knowledge that comes through a personal relationship with another. We trace such a growing and deepening relationship through various stages in our human relationships, and so it is with God. So Paul prayed for the Christians at Ephesus that God would give them 'a spirit of wisdom and revelation' in the knowledge of God the Father of glory, 'having the eyes of their hearts enlightened' (Ephesians 1.17–18).

Christ and the Father

But how on earth can we suppose that such a relationship is possible with the all-transcendent God? There are two answers which perhaps we have never taken seriously enough, in spite of the fact that such a relationship of intimacy was explicitly revealed as being deeply desired on his part by Christ himself, who, as St Francis said, 'died for love of our love'. In the first place, Jesus tells us repeatedly that he chooses to reveal God his Father to those he has chosen. And second, and perhaps more wonderfully, he has expressed his desire for an intimate relationship with us and we with and in him, so that we can be brought into the life of the Trinity by the Holy Spirit who is given to us.

Such an intimate relationship is spelled out in no uncertain terms in John's Gospel – the Gospel inspired specifically by the one who, humanly speaking, was the closest to Jesus, always so memorably referred to as 'the disciple whom Jesus loved' and who rested on the bosom (heart to heart) of Jesus in the intimacy of the Last Supper – a picture that was to be etched deeply into the collective memory of the whole apostolic band. It's as though John is perceived as being singled out as the beloved disciple, who rested on the bosom of Jesus, and as such reflects in human terms the relationship of Jesus with his Father and ours. John goes on to tell us that Jesus was and is 'close to the Father's heart'. In all of this we have an icon which points those with eyes to see to the kind of 'knowledge' that comes from such a heart-to-heart relationship.

So on that same evening, in the Upper Room, surrounded by his chosen disciples, Jesus finally 'comes out' about his relation-ship with his Father and his deeply desired relationship with those who seek to follow him. At table, with the beloved disciple on his breast and surrounded by his disciples, Jesus opens his heart to them and to all who will come after them. 'In a little while the world will no longer see me, but you will see me; because I live, you also will live. On that day you will know that I am in my Father, and you in me, and I in you' (John 14.19–20). And again: 'Those who love me will keep my word, and my Father will love them, and we will come to them and make our home with them' (John 14.23). And yet again, as though to drive all this home: 'As the Father has loved me, so I have loved you; abide in my love' (John 15.9).

We read these overwhelming words of Jesus only in John's Gospel – the last of the Gospels, written several decades later. In that Upper Room on that night of all nights to remember, it would have been impossible for those bewildered disciples to take all this in – with the possible exception of the beloved disciple, so close to the heart of Jesus. It was only after Pentecost and the coming of the Holy Spirit, whom Jesus had promised would bring back to the remembrance of those disciples all that he had taught them, that they would experience for themselves the overwhelming truth and power of what Jesus had opened up for them. It was all too much for them at the time, and it's all too much for us now.

Only with the coming of the Holy Spirit into our hearts and lives can we possibly make those promises and words of Jesus our own – not only in prayer, but also in our whole way of life. God in Christ has opened his heart to us, and now he longs for us to open our hearts to him, as we grow ever more deeply into a relationship with the Father, through the Son and in the love and life of the Spirit of Love who draws us and binds us into the life of the Blessed Trinity. So it's no longer a matter of being merely 'servants' of God who do not really know what on earth God is getting up to! We are now drawn by the Holy Spirit into an intimate relationship beyond our wildest understanding or imagining if we take Jesus at his word and take his word into our hearts.

We are children of God, by adoption and grace, with Jesus as our brother, with the same Father in the one universal family of God. When Jesus was asked to give a lesson on prayer, he urged us to begin, not with 'My Father', but rather with 'Our Father'. This has wild implications, and not only for prayer and praying. In effect, Jesus is saying, 'When you pray, always pray together with me your brother, and let us pray together to our Father.

Such teaching and practice is even more revolutionary when we consider that Jesus was teaching this to Jews, for whom the very name of God was unmentionable. Now we are instructed by Jesus, together with him as our brother, and through his Holy Spirit, to address the unspeakable and unnamed God 'Abba' – 'Daddy'. To Jews, as well as to Muslims and many others, such a form of address would be little short of blasphemy.

Perhaps something similar to this developing relationship with God 'our Father' is mirrored in the maturing relationship between children and their parents. Often, as children grow up, they become the friends of their parents as mature men and women. It would seem from the teaching of Jesus that God also desires that amazing development towards what we might want to call a mature relationship with God our Father.

Such claims distinguish the Christian faith from any other religious faith in the world. And all this by way of gift – freely given, unearned and clearly undeserved. This maturing relationship, which will never be fully realized in this world, is what the ancient Fathers of the Church – especially the Eastern Fathers – term as our 'divinization' or 'deification'. St Athanasius (296–373) claimed that Christ 'became man that we might become divine' or, as I would prefer, that we might 'share in the divine life of the Godhead'. Lest we should think that this is an eccentric presumption of the Eastern Churches, we have the words of St Thomas Aquinas to reassure western Christians of the same amazing reality: 'The only begotten Son of God, wishing to enable us to share in his divinity, assumed our nature, so that by becoming man, he might make men gods.' And lest you should think that such a presumption as sharing in the 'divine nature' is theologically over the top, listen again to the witness of scripture. 'His divine power has given us everything needed for life and godliness, through the knowledge of him who called us by his own glory and goodness. Thus he has given us, through these things, his precious and very great promises, so that through them you . . . may become participants in the divine nature' (2 Peter 1.3f).

Such theology underlies symbolically the words of the priest in the liturgy, as he mixes the water and the wine, praying that 'by the mystery of this water and wine, may we come to share in the divinity of Christ who humbled himself to share in our humanity'. Nothing less than that is the direction of the spiritual journey and the goal of contemplative prayer, fully realized in contemplative worship and living.

One last and nagging qualification in all of this. All that is said here is most certainly not just for monks and nuns or 'professionals', so to speak. It is nothing more or less than the full realization of our baptismal life when the little 'pilot light' of the Holy Spirit was first ignited within us. Subsequently, the life of prayer and the indwelling of the Holy Spirit enables that same little 'pilot light' to burst into a living flame to become the fire of God's unconditional and passionate love, burning brightly yet not consumed, as 'we daily increase in his Holy Spirit more and more' (Book of Common Prayer, Confirmation Service).

Notes

1   Kenneth Leech, *True Prayer: An Introduction to Christian Spirituality* (Sheldon Press, 1980), p. 11.
2   Thomas Green, SJ, *When the Well Runs Dry* (Ave Maria Press, 1979), p. 11.
3   Antoine de Saint-Exupery, *The Little Prince* (Wordsworth Editions, 1995), p. 82.

9

Opening Up to God

Removing the barriers and road-blocks

Although God has made it perfectly clear, at the very least through the Incarnation of Christ – Jesus Christ, who is 'bone of our bone and flesh of our flesh' – that he deeply desires to incorporate the experience of what it is to be truly human into his own divine life and into the fellowship and shared life of the Blessed Trinity, most of us find the reality of this amazing new revelation much to take in. From God's point of view, all the barriers between heaven and earth, the creation and the Creator, and specifically between what is essentially human and what is divine – all those barriers from God's side have been broken down once and for all. Love 'bids us welcome' on every front and without reserve.

Yet although Christ stands at the door of our hearts, longing to enter, 'to come in and eat' with us and we with him (Revelation 3.20), the entrance of our 'courteous Lord', as Dame Julian of Norwich refers to Christ, is never a forced entrance. As the famous painting by Holman Hunt, 'The Light of the World', so strikingly portrays, the handle of that door to the human heart, is significantly placed on the inside, with the implication that everything depends upon our willingness to open up to the life and love of the Holy Spirit of God with open hearts and open minds. For as Jesus reminded his hearers, 'The Kingdom of God is within' (Luke 17.21). Quoting from Deuteronomy, Paul picks up on this understanding of the interior presence of Christ: 'What does it say? "The word is near you, on your lips and in your heart" (that is, the word of faith)' (Romans 10.8).

God has taken the initiative in every respect, and not least when it comes to our response in prayer and worship. All the barriers between God and ourselves, including the barriers resulting from Adam's disobedience and misguided knowledge, have been crossed from God's side by the Incarnation of Christ. For Christ, 'though he was in the form of God, did not regard equality with God as something to be exploited, but emptied himself, taking the form of a slave, being born in human likeness. And being found in human form' (Philippians 2.6, 7). We express the staggering theological implications of all that is implied by the Incarnation in the more accessible words of the well-known hymn, 'Thou didst leave thy throne and thy kingly crown when thou camest to earth for me . . . O come to my heart Lord Jesus, make room in my heart for Thee.'[1]

Conversely and equally wonderful is the doctrine of the Ascension of Christ and his return to the Father, by which Jesus opened up a new and living way into the heart of God himself, where he has gone to prepare a place for us, that where Christ reigns we may find our true and lasting home within the heart of God, in union with the Father and the Son and in the shared life of the Holy Spirit. In his Ascension, Christ retained his humanity and took it and, by implication, us, back into the very heart of God himself. Unlike the gods in Greek mythology who briefly visit the earth, to 'flirt' with our humanity, Jesus, as the Church teaches and as scripture explicitly endorses, 'took our humanity as never more to lay it down'. The wounds of love which the risen Lord showed to his disciples are for eternity etched on our divinized humanity in the heart of God. There is a wounded man in the heavens! So the way is open, in both directions, in the words of Newman's motto: 'Heart speaks to heart.'

Like that younger son in the parable of the Prodigal Son, when I 'come to myself' (my true self), I will know where my true home is and where I truly belong as well as where the Father longs to welcome me, along with all his sons and daughters, on my return journey from that 'far country' of alienation and isolation. Also, from that same parable, we learn of how the loving Father goes out of his way and 'runs' more than half-way to meet us in Jesus Christ. And better still – and to the extent that we have the mind of Christ – we can be assured of the way home to true, abundant and eternal life, all of which is revealed to those with 'eyes to see and ears to hear', by the promptings of the Holy Spirit who continually brings the words and teachings of Christ into the here-and-now and wherever we are on the spiritual journey. Furthermore, all this still holds true even if, like those two disciples on the road to Emmaus, we are going in the wrong direction.

So all the road-blocks on the road of our spiritual journeys, where they still exist, are of our making. The first and most common barrier to the deepening of our relationship with the true and living God through prayer, is our own – frequently subconscious – reluctance to desire truly such a relationship. A heart must be really listening, really wanting the truth – in a word, really wanting God.

> The difficulty is that we do not want him. We want our own version of him, one we can, so to speak, carry around in our pockets rather as some superstitious people carry around a charm.We can hold endless, loving conversations with this one, feel we have an intimate understanding with him, we can tell him our troubles, ask for his approbation and admiration, consult him about all our affairs and decisions and get the answer we want, and this God of ours has almost nothing to do with God.[2]

There is another barrier and barricade from behind which we seek to evade the full impact of God's loving invitation to come out from our chosen place of hiding. Those of us who are used to being in control and managing all that we undertake, want to be successful and become experts in whatever we take up. During our school days we 'dropped' those subjects we were not very good at, in order to 'specialize' in the subjects of our choosing and in which we supposed that we would be successful. However, we need to know from the outset, not only that prayer is not primarily what *we* do, but also that we will never be experts in prayer. The spiritual life is essentially for amateurs, in the real meaning of that word – namely, for those who 'love' what they do for its own sake, rather than for those who are successful at what they do. True love needs no justification. Prayer is not a technique that can be mastered: it is all about a relationship which needs nurturing and deepening in good and bad times alike. There is always the temptation that we will want to control our relationship with God in the same way that we seek to be in control of other relationships, turning them on and off when and as we want, applying many and any well-tried techniques in those areas of our lives which by definition defy managing and controlling.

The building-blocks of intimacy

In an age of mobile phones, laptops and i-Pods, many people today are imprisoned within the expectations of permanent availability – always on call, 24/7 as we often say.

> Amid the glittering promise of our new technologies and the wondrous potential of our scientific gains, we are nurturing a culture of social diffusion, intellectual fragmentation, sensory detachment. In this new world something is amiss. And that something is attention.

'Attention', Maggie Jackson rightly maintains, is the 'building block of intimacy, wisdom and cultural progress. It's as though today the human self is collectively suffering from what has been diagnosed as the attention deficit syndrome.'[3]

In 1890 the psychologist and philosopher William James rightly claimed that in choosing to give attention to something or somebody 'implies withdrawal from some things in order to deal effectively with others, and is a condition which has a real opposite in the confused, dazed, scatter-brained state which in French is called *distraction*'.[4]

Solitude

'"Come away to a deserted place all by yourselves and rest awhile" said Jesus. For many were coming and going, and they had no leisure even to eat' (Mark 6.31). Such was the explicit admonition of Jesus to disciples 'beside themselves' after their frenetic activity in ministry and mission. Jesus has the same admonition for all would-be disciples in every age and, by no means least, in our own age – for clergy and laity alike.

> Our society is a dangerous network of domination and manipulation in which we can easily get entangled and lose our soul. The call of Jesus is to let our false, compulsive self be transformed into the new self of Jesus Christ . . . Solitude is the furnace in which this transformation takes place. Without solitude we remain victims of our society and continue to be entangled in the illusions of the false self.[5]

So, when Jesus wanted to reveal the glory of himself in relationship to his Father and ours to that inner cabinet of his apostolic band, on the Mountain of Transfiguration, we read that he led those three disciples, Peter, James and John, 'up a mountain *apart* by themselves'. It would seem that God is no exhibitionist, so that his self-revelations are ring-fenced to prevent the voyeurism which is so compulsively bent on 'kicks' – spiritual or otherwise. Furthermore, Luke frequently refers to the practice of Jesus himself, when praying to his Father. Usually, he would withdraw either to the desert or to 'a lonely place apart', generally either very early in the morning, or in the silence of the night.

Solitude is indeed a precious commodity in our own day and especially in the inner cities with their 'crowded clangour' as well as in the course of family life on a working day, when the children need to be taken to school, or when the dog needs to go for a walk, only to be followed by journeying to work on crowded trains and buses from the earliest hours of the day. Space, silence and solitude are truly at a high premium in today's workaday world.

So it is that there is a new and urgent need for sacred space. For as parks are the lungs of a crowded city, in a similar way there is an equal need for church buildings to be open and silent as sanctuaries of sanity, affording another dimension to our overcrowded lives and not least during the working week. It is so sad to see locked churches, closed to the real needs of over-populated cities, and apparently indifferent to the very purposes for which they were originally built, namely as affording 'sacred space' not only to 'club members' and churchgoers at 'club hours', but open for anybody and everybody as needed. Clergy and ministers alike should know that they are the custodians of these cherished places which should symbolize in their 'openness' the patient waiting of a God who longs with deep desire to draw us apart, both with himself and for himself alone.

But the solitude that is such an essential building-block for intimacy and openness to the Other, must be distinguished from that solitude regarded as the right to privacy. For solitude, properly understood, is not the place where our so-called 'private life' is cosseted and massaged. Far from it. It is the place of painful and costly transformation:

> In solitude I get rid of my scaffolding: no friends to talk with, no telephone calls to make, no meetings to attend, no music to entertain, no books to distract, just me – naked, vulnerable, weak, sinful, deprived, broken – nothing. It is this nothingness

that I have to face in my solitude, a nothingness so dreadful that everything in me wants to run to my friends, my work, and my distractions so that I can forget my nothingness and make myself believe that I am worth something.[6]

Silence

As solitude is the order of the day, so is the silence that should accompany it. Silence is indeed a rare commodity in today's world. It needs to be both sought out as well as practised. Of course it is helpful if, in our times set aside for prayer, we can get away to a place that is no longer invaded by the sounds of the city, with the endless music-players, or the piped music which pervades and invades nearly all public places, whether in restaurants, shopping malls or on television screens, in taxis or blaring out from outdoor parties in gardens or parks, or just those overheard conversations on mobile phones, on buses and public transport. It's refreshing to see that on some trains there are special 'Quiet Compartments' offered, but equally fascinating to see how often so many people simply cannot go for a whole journey without talking trivia through all the latest forms of telecommunication. One thing is clear: noise pollution is here to stay.

Yet in seeking silence we do not mean only the absence of external noise or speech. Most people, and especially those who live alone, 'talk to themselves'; and even if we are not afflicted in that way, then it is so often at times of external silence that many of us break out with an incessant interior chatter which, as one of the Fathers of the Church puts it, is 'like monkeys in a banana tree'! We desperately need therefore to practise interior silence as the ground bass for inner stillness, and not least when everything around us is agitated and noisy, frenetic and seeking to arrest our attention.

'Be still, then, and know that I am God,' says the psalmist (Psalm 46.10). In the Latin of the Vulgate it is rendered '*Vacate et videte*'. Interestingly, a possible translation might read – 'Take a break or a vacation and stop playing at God – let God be God for a little while.' 'Chill out' even!

Building our 'enclosure'

Clearly, all these prerequisites for deepening our relationship between our true selves and the living God require a discipline and the determination to make time as well as space to come before the Lord and to open ourselves to the inner workings of the Spirit of the living God, in order that he may work his pleasure deep within us and always essentially from the inside out. This reworking is something so much more than cosmetic or skin-deep, quite unlike all our self-help methods of reinventing ourselves.

Our first knee-jerk response to this challenge is to plead a busy life with too many demands upon our time and energies. Yet we need to counter this claim. After all, the present cult of the gym and the prime place many busy people give to 'working out', surely indicates that, as the saying goes, 'Where there's a will, there's a way.' Experience over many years, frequently through failure, nevertheless convinces me that we all need specific times – and quality time at that – set aside, by force of habit, for the things in our lives that are really important to us. It won't just happen by doing what comes naturally. Nothing can be generalized until it is first particularized.

> Whatever we may say about particular times and methods of prayer, this much is essential, that each day should have some dedicated silence in it. This is the gift of our time to God. We are to put ourselves at God's disposal in the quietness. The prayer will be dispersed throughout the day, throughout our activity, but there will be some dedicated spaces of silence.[7]

As regularity is the clue to a healthy physical life, so it is that regularity, in what we often speak of as a 'rule of life', ensures a similar regularity and provides a framework to the day, so that we can be sustained regularly with our 'daily bread'. The fatal thing is to pray only as and when we feel like it, as though God were at our beck and call, waiting for us to 'sign in' and 'call up'. We demean our friends and others if we call them fitfully, as and when we happen to want something: good and deep relation-ships are not built in that way. Rather, we make time, as we say, for things and people we consider important.

> Every Christian by virtue of the grace of baptism, *has* the vocation to oneness with the Father through Jesus Christ, in the Holy Spirit. Everyone needs some kind of practice in order to accomplish this vocation. Obviously a rule of life cannot be as detailed for those living in the world as it is for people living in a monastery. But everyone has to build his or her own kind of enclosure as far as one's duties allow, by setting aside a certain amount of time every day for prayer and spiritual reading. Also, perhaps, one may dedicate a day every month, and a week every year, to being alone with the Lord.[8]

Some form of daily routine which affords prime time set aside for openness to God in prayer really does change the outcome of the rest of the day. The day that begins with prayer and openness to God is really a very different day from that kind of day which could be described as just 'one damn thing after another'. And furthermore, I have found that, after a while, when a time of prayer early in the day has become habitual, I really do begin to feel drawn to do it; and certainly if I do not make that time, I know in my inner self that something is missing, as I set out to work.

With the habitual practice of early morning prayer, times of waiting for a bus, or sitting on the bus, or indeed during any time of enforced waiting, whether for a train or at an airport, rather than perceived as 'killing time', I find I almost subconsciously return to a still centre within me, which I'm convinced is the direct result of the specific time of prayer earlier in the day. Furthermore, what I would perhaps otherwise have written off as purely coincidental has about it something of what I feel compelled to call 'providential', with all the quiet, inner assurance that comes with such a different outlook on the events of a so-called ordinary day. Perhaps what we pass off as 'coincidence' is God's way of remaining anonymous.

Now of course it has to be admitted that much of what I'm saying demands a counter-cultural outlook on life. The spiritual journey is indeed a 'road less travelled', for to follow in this way necessarily requires us to 'walk by faith, not by sight' (2 Corinthians 5.7). 'The only ultimate disaster that can befall us', said Malcolm Muggeridge, 'is to feel ourselves at home on earth.' For there is a sense in which authentic Christian disciples are never quite at home in this world. When the Jews were in exile in Babylon, the psalmist exploded into melancholy tones, expressing in the power of poetry the experience of exile: 'How shall we sing the Lord's song upon an alien soil' (Psalm 137.4). How indeed? For, as St Paul put it: 'Our citizenship is in heaven' (Philippians 3.20).

The 'culture of God' will always be misunderstood from the point of view of a secular culture, as being counter-cultural at best and at worst as sheer 'foolishness' by many, and not least in an age which measures everything in terms of material gain, achievement and physical well-being. We will need to belong to a community which is also committed to the spiritual journey and all that it involves. That is where our corporate life in the fellowship of the Church has its essential place, whether expressed in home groups, Bible study groups or prayer groups as the outworking of the gathered Church in worship on the Lord's Day, at the Lord's own service. In this way, the regular practice of personal prayer complements and supplements liturgical, corporate prayer and worship. 'In the liturgy, we are lifted out of our anxieties about our private prayer and when we pray the prayer of the whole Church'.[9]

But we must not seek 'the pay-off' of the practice of prayer, whether corporate or personal, in the terms of the world. There will indeed be a 'pay-off' ('rewarded openly' as Christ promised), for, as we shall see, the workings of God are essentially hidden before they are revealed, like the leaven hidden, or like the seed that is sown and grows in ways we do not perceive until the day of the harvest.

Notes

1   *New English Hymnal* (The Canterbury Press, 1986), No. 465.
2   Sister Ruth Burrows OCD, *Essence of Prayer* (Burns & Oates, 2006), p. 14.
3   Maggie Jackson, *Distracted: The Erosion and the Coming Dark Age* (Prometheus Books, 2008), p. 13.
4   William James (ed. Frederick Burkhardt), *The Principles of Psychology* (Harvard University Press, 1981), p. 381.
5   Henri Nouwen, *The Way of the Heart* (HarperCollins, 1991), p. 20ff.
6   Nouwen, *The Way of the Heart*, p. 27.
7   Eric Symes Abbott, *Invitations to Prayer* (Forward Movement Publications, 1989), p. 37.
8   Thomas Keating, *The Heart of the World: An Introduction to Contemplative Christianity* (Crossroad Publishing, 1981), p. 11.
9   Abbott, *Invitations to Prayer*, p. 43.

10

The Prayer of Transformation

Faith or certainty

'The spiritual journey', writes Thomas Keating 'is a call into the unknown.' He further claims that 'the only way to get' to that place or state where God wants us to be – the location and ultimate 'home' of our true self – 'is to consent not to know. The desire or the demand for certitude is an obstacle to launching full sail on the ocean of trust.'[1]

This quest for certainty – some might even say 'obsession' with the need for certainty – especially in our own day, together with its illusions of security, is the bane of so much that masquerades as religion or faith. Certainty is the very opposite of true faith, and, necessarily by definition, borders dangerously on idolatry. In reality, the posturing of certainty is far more destructive than healthy doubt or an open-minded agnosticism with the ability simply to say: 'God knows! I don't know.' At the very heart of what we like to call Abrahamic faith is the ability to trust in a person, rather than bolstering our insecurity with the supposedly unquestionable doctrinal summaries of creeds and dogmas.

It is significant that Christianity, Judaism and Islam alike look to Abraham as the father of true faith, precisely because his faith manifested itself as total trust in the call of God, even when he could not possibly have known the outcome of all that he was being asked to do. In commonsense terms and certainly in prospect, all that God was asking him to do must have appeared as utter madness. At the age of 75, when most of us would think it was well time to settle down, take out the carpet-slippers and put our feet up – it was precisely at that age that the Lord God called Abraham to 'rise up', to pull up his tent-pegs, put on his walking boots and move out. The Church (*ecclesia*, in Latin) by definition should embody that same quality of faith and trust in so far as all Christians have been 'called out', in faith and trust to 'come out'. Such is the nature of true discipleship, resourced by prayer, and tested in the laboratory of daily life.

'Then the Lord told Abram, "Leave your country, your relatives, and your father's house, and go to the land that I will show you . . . I will bless you"' (Genesis 12.1–2). God was asking well-known, old Abram (his original name) to let go and to leave behind him everything that had helped to make Abram the kind of person everyone knew him to be – namely, 'Good *old* Abram'!

But in order for 'good old Abram' to be changed into the Godlike, holy *new Abraham*, the new man would need to break with the old, to step out into the totally unknown territory, culture, language and environment of a very different kingdom. When perhaps his wife or kindred asked him for directions and for those other useful kinds of details one usually researches before setting out on any kind of journey for the first time, old Abram would necessarily have had to reply, something along the lines: 'God alone knows. I don't know! All I do know is that our future is all in God's hands.'

So, in the epistle to the Hebrews, the author traces the 'family tree' of this Abrahamic faith – a faith that is ready and willing to trust and believe without knowing, understanding or being in control of the foreseeable outcome – a trust that is willing 'to walk by faith and not by sight', let alone foresight (2 Corinthians 5.7). It is with such faith, like the 'new' Abraham of Genesis, that we, together with all those who have followed in the way of Abraham, are eternally blessed and recreated into the holy people of God, re-fashioned and remade both in his likeness as well as his image. But, from start to finish we need to rest assured that it's all in God's hands, and most especially when it comes to prayer and praying in the Spirit of God.

The divine initiative of love

Perhaps it is as we grow in our relationship with God through prayer that such faith and trust is most put to the test, especially for those of us who always want things on our terms, in our way and in our time. Initially, it would seem that our gracious God willingly meets us and connects with us on our terms, our turf and our territory, where we are known and where we are, to some extent, 'at home': in contemporary jargon, in our 'comfort zone'. After all, that is what the Incarnation is all about. God in Christ connects with our humanity with all its limitations: the limitations of a particular language, a particular gender, a particular nationality, and all this within the limitations of the world-view of his day. Admittedly, it would seem that Christ, in his Incarnation and his earthly ministry, found all these limitations and restrictions incredibly frustrating. 'I came to bring fire to the earth, and how I wish it were already kindled! I have a baptism with which to be baptized, and what stress I am under until it is completed' (Luke 12.49–50).

Since God in Christ has come more than halfway to connect with us where and as we are, it follows that the first step in prayer must be our willing response to come to him just as we are, without any kind of 'religious' veneer, either in our language or in a religiously sanitized self.

On our side prayer is simply being there: open, exposed, inviting God to do all God wants. Prayer is not *our* activity, *our* getting in touch with God, *our* coming to grips with or making ourselves desirable to God.[2]

The Gospel record vividly tells us that Christ touched the untouchables and the unclean, much of course to the outrage of the 'religious' leaders. This alone should reassure us that we do not need to wait until we have improved or cleaned up, before we can approach the Lord in prayer. There is a natural hesitancy born of our original religious upbringing, and indeed in much that has been proclaimed by the Church, that would tempt us to draw back – 'guiltie of dust and sin' as George Herbert puts it.

From the outset we need to counter this self-consciousness, however understandable it may be. We shall never live as we pray unless we first learn to pray as we live, with all the contradictions of our daily manner of life. No one should pretend that it is anything other than painful to come into the presence of the Lord, knowing full well that we have betrayed in what we have done or said the One who truly loves us. Yet it is in precisely that place of pain that Christ can heal us: he goes straight to the wound, but only if we are willing to uncover it and expose ourselves to Christ's healing touch. In the New Testament, Jesus is never shocked by our sins, though he is frequently on record as being shocked by our fear.

'There is no fear in love,' says St John, 'but perfect love casts out fear; for fear has to do with punishment, and whoever fears has not reached perfection in love' (1 John 4.18). At the same time, however, we should not 'presume' on that unconditional love of God for us. As it says in the 'Prayer of Humble Access' from the Book of Common Prayer, we can never come before the Lord, 'trusting in our own righteousness', let alone by asserting our own worthiness of such loving and all-embracing acceptance. The only fear in our deepening relationship with God should be that 'fear' which is born of 'awe' arising from the overwhelming knowledge that we are truly loved by the One who knows us as we truly are and yet who still persists in loving us 'to the uttermost' (John 13.1). It is indeed an awesome thing 'to fall into the hands of the living God' (Hebrews 10.31), yet at the same time we should rest assured that there is no safer place in the world to be in.

Furthermore, our own experience would tell us that when we love someone or know that someone truly loves us, we naturally want to try to please them. So 'the love of Christ controls us' (2 Corinthians 5.14). It is love rather than fear that should condition and motivate our behaviour. Sadly, however, frequently throughout history in commending morality and Christian behaviour, the Church has resorted to preaching the fear of hell, whereas it should have been far more concerned to put up-front God's exceedingly great love for us, exemplified by Christ in his teaching, his life, suffering and death. The whole purpose of Christ's journey from heaven to earth, from his Father's side to be on our side and to be beside us (Emmanuel – 'God with us') is to meet us where we are, in order that he might take us (draw us) to where he wishes us to be: to take us from what we know or think we know, to what we do not yet know; accepting us for what we are, but in order to remake us into what he has always desired us to be. 'And if I go and prepare a place for you, I will come again and will take you to myself, that where I am, there you may be also' (John 14.3).

Love that cannot be put into words

So all true prayer is a response of love to love, in the love of the Holy Spirit. 'In this is love, not that we loved God, but that he loved us' (1 John 4.10). St Theresa reminds us that 'prayer is not thinking much; prayer is loving much'. In true love, of course, although the words and vocabulary of love in the early stages have a place in close relationships, further on and as we grow in love, words begin to take second place. Communication through words often moves comfortably into 'communion' experienced in silence. For those of us who are articulate in speech, for wordsmiths or for those of us who just like the sound of our own voice, it is difficult to escape from the prison house of our claustrophobic vocabulary, even while knowing intuitively that the deeper the experience, the more difficult it is to put it into words.

There is both loss and gain from translating the words of the liturgy into the vernacular. There is of course a place for 'following the service' from a printed service sheet or a prayer book. There is also, however, a place for the use of a language (like Latin in the Middle Ages) which bypasses the processes of the mind precisely because the action of the liturgy has 'overtaken' speech. Communion is deeper than mere communication.

For many people, the gift of speaking-in-tongues and the release which it brings really can represent a further step in the life of prayer. (Of course, like every other gift or indeed anything else in this world, the gift of speaking-in-tongues does have a downside in so far as it can be accompanied by spiritual pride, as Paul was swift to point out to the infant church in Corinth.)

Yet, on balance, the charismatic movement has proved to be a great blessing in all branches of the Church, and especially in the life of churches over-dominated by intellectual control systems and verbiage. The breath and wind of the Spirit gently bends our tendencies to rigidity as well as those recurring temptations to revert from grace to law in a formalism and legalism that are the very opposite of the freedom of the gospel. Structure and form, like the spine, are given in order to enable spontaneity, setting us free to bend without breaking. Paradoxically, it is the structure of the spine that gives us the flexibility to dance! In many ways, speaking-in-tongues is a kind of love language and can serve as another stepping-stone to a deeper life of prayer. It can put the articulate and active side of the brain on hold, so to speak, while the intuitive and reflective (non-verbal) side of the brain opens up in 'wonder, love and praise'. In many ways we should regard 'speaking-in-tongues' not so much as a thing in itself and for itself, to be grasped and coveted, but rather as a stepping-stone to the more contemplative, wordless prayer of loving regard.

Yet in whatever way God provides, we will need to move in

our 'prayer language' from words to beyond words; from seeing the printed words on the page of scripture, to listening for the Living Word – Jesus – in an ever-deepening relationship with the risen Lord. And all this is revealed, as Christ promised, by the Holy Spirit which he has given us and in which we should 'daily increase' until we finally come to the Father in the culture of the Kingdom of God. There and there alone, we shall know as we are known: our old, false self having been transformed into the new Godlike self, with that new name that finally reveals who we are and always were intended by God to be.

Knowing and not knowing

The spiritual journey is necessarily a bumpy ride. Those words of Jesus to his disciples on the eve of his crucifixion can apply in a different context and at various points on our spiritual journey. 'A little while, and you will no longer see me, and again a little while and you will see me' (John 16.16). There are times when we see the road ahead opening up clearly, when it really seems as though we 'know' God and therefore that we know a little bit more about ourselves, as the clouds clear and there is a momentary beam of sunlight breaking through – a particular phrase from scripture lights up or when we have a warm experience of God's presence with us and in us. Then again, however, the clouds roll in and we do not know where we are going, what to say or, indeed, who we truly are, let alone who God is.

Prayer and scripture

'I still have many things to say to you, but you cannot bear them now', Jesus said to those bewildered disciples in their hesitating first steps. 'When the Spirit of truth comes, he will guide you into all the truth . . . he will take what is mine and declare it to you' (John 16.12f). This promise of Christ presupposes that we will let the Holy Spirit lead us in prayer. All our prayer times demand that we begin by opening ourselves to the Holy Spirit and by invoking the Holy Spirit to illuminate the flight path and the launch pad. We might want to use the well-known opening prayer from the Book of Common Prayer at the beginning of the Eucharist: 'Almighty God, to whom all hearts are open, all desires known and from whom no secrets are hidden: Cleanse the thoughts of our hearts by the inspiration of your Holy Spirit, that we may perfectly love . . .' At other times a prayer song* invoking the Holy Spirit of just a phrase from scripture: 'Speak, LORD, for your servant is listening' (1 Samuel 3.9).

Then perhaps, we can use a passage of scripture, preferably read aloud, slowly and several times.† After all, as the psalmist says, 'Your word is a lamp to my feet and a light to my path' (Psalm 119.105). So let scripture be exactly that, but no more than that. As we have seen in the first part of this book, both the scriptures and the sacraments are icons, not idols: they should not draw us to themselves. Rather, they point beyond themselves to the One who is himself the Way, the Truth and the Life. *Through* both the scriptures and the breaking of the Bread, the risen Christ reveals himself to us as he did to those two disciples on the road to Emmaus. But that revelation was and is *through* scripture and *through* the sacraments, for Christ is not to be trapped within either of them, let alone within any limited, human understanding seeking to explain them. Both the scriptures and the sacraments are rightly termed as *means* of grace – means and not ends.

In this way, after a while, the centre of our consciousness needs to move from the mind with its own particular kind of knowledge – albeit limited – to the heart, the seat of our desires, yearnings and longings with a stretch beyond its reach, into the mystery of a relationship in which we are content not to know.‡

---

*'More Prayer Songs', CD by the Revd Soon Han Choi, available through www.spapray.org.uk. See Appendix B, p. 143.
†See Appendix A for more about this way of reading scripture – spiritual reading or 'lectio divina'.
‡See Appendix B for more about the practice of Centering Prayer and Contemplative Prayer.

This is that other kind of knowledge, the knowledge received through a relationship beyond words, as we rest in the silence, content simply to be in the presence of God, not 'thinking much' at all but responding to love with love.

A prayer word

Of course the wandering thoughts will come in their plenty, but with the repeated use of what we call a little prayer word – 'Jesus', 'Abba', 'Father', 'Amen' or whatever – we should not try to suppress those wandering thoughts, for that only reinforces them with extra energy. Rather, by returning gently to our repeated prayer word, we simply let go of them rather than chasing after them. The repetition of the prayer word is likened by one of the Fathers of the Eastern Church

> . . . to the beating of wings by which a bird rises into the air. It must never be laboured and forced, or hurried or in the nature of a flapping. It must be gentle, easy and – let us give to this word its deepest meaning – graceful. When the bird has reached the desired height it glides in its flight, and only beats its wings from time to time in order to stay in the air . . . The repetition will only be resumed when other thoughts threaten to crowd out the thought of Jesus. Then the invocation will start again in order to gain fresh impetus.[3]

In all of this we must no longer seek to be in control, which, for control freaks as many of us are, constitutes a real stumbling-block. Prayer is not primarily what we do, although at the outset it seems a little as though that is the case. On the contrary, prayer is what God does in the eternal dialogue between the Father and the Son, between the Lover and the Beloved. As we open our hearts in faith we are drawn into that relationship and shared life by the Holy Spirit of love. In that way, as brothers and sisters *of* Christ and *in* Christ we are presented and re-presented to his Father and ours. 'So come to the Father, through Jesus the Son, and praise him, O praise him, great things he hath done.'

Of course there will be the dry times when we feel that nothing is happening and when we are tempted to suppose that the whole exercise is only little less than a waste of time. Perhaps we tell ourselves, 'Isn't it time to get back into the driving seat and get a "hands on" approach to this whole business of prayer?' As such we need to recognize that reaction for what it is, namely, the 'old self' – the left side of the brain – reasserting itself again. Yet such times can be, and often are, those very times when we are imperceptibly growing in prayer. At such times the Holy Spirit is taking a further initiative, probing, like drilling for oil in the depths of the ocean of our subconscious at a level far deeper than our senses, feelings or perceptions. For God is not *in* any of those, although he conde-scends to come to us and to speak to us *through* our senses as well as other means of sensory perception.

> To repeat a mantra (i.e. a short prayer) can be an excellent way of helping us to focus on receiving God's love. So, too, can reflection on a Scripture text. Most of us certainly need some support to keep us there. But we must learn to distin-guish between making use of a support and of substituting the support for prayer. Keeping our deepest heart exposed, refusing to usurp God's place by making ourselves the agent, the giver, will mean that, most often, we have no sense of having prayed well or having prayed at all.[4]

So, by grace and grace alone, we grow, unselfconsciously, into the likeness of the true and living God, while at the same time growing more and more distinctively into our own true selves, as God first imagined us to be. But we need always to remember that 'it is the Lord's doing and it is marvellous in our eyes'.

So if this is what we mean by prayer – a kind of resting in God and waiting upon him – then of course St Paul is right on the button when he admits that we do not know how to pray as we ought. But, thanks be to God, we do not need to worry too much about divine etiquette! The Holy Spirit 'helps us in our weakness', and therein lies our strength. 'That very Spirit', says St Paul, 'intercedes with sighs too deep for words.' So who are we to worry too much about being 'lost for words'? And all this as God probes and 'searches the heart, praying and interceding for us', but always 'according to the will of God' and not according to our limited agendas (Romans 8.26).

> Meanwhile, the moment we get tired in waiting, God's Spirit is right alongside, helping us along. If we don't know how or what to pray, it doesn't matter. He does our praying in and for us, making prayer out of our wordless sighs, our aching groans. He knows us far better than we know ourselves, knows our pregnant condition, and keeps us present before God. That's why we can be so sure that every detail in our lives of love for God is worked into something good.[5]

Notes

1   Thomas Keating, *Invitation to Love* (Continuum, 1992), p. 75.
2   Sister Ruth Burrows OCD, *Essence of Prayer* (Burns & Oates, 2006), p. 28.
3   Martin Smith, *The Word is Very Near You: A Guide to Praying with Scripture* (Cowley Publications, 1989), pp. 121–2.
4   Burrows, *Essence of Prayer*, p. 7.
5   Eugene Peterson, *'Conversations': The Message Bible with its Translator* (NavPress, 2005), Romans 8.26f., p. 1752.

11

The New Creation

In the recovery programme for Alcoholics Anonymous the first step to sobriety is taken when addicts openly admit that they are powerless to help themselves; that their life has become unmanageable and that they now accept the need to reach out to a higher power than themselves. Such a step and such an admission generally comes very painfully and only after years of denial. The problem for addicts is only further compounded, as long as they seek to eradicate their addiction solely by exercising their own willpower. While such a response and such a course of action would seem in the eyes of most people to be commendable, in practice it only serves to reinforce the illusion that it is by our own strength of will that we are able to overcome our failings and weaknesses and that self-improvement is within our own control.

Yet in practice, through bitter experience and after many failures, the realization inevitably dawns, informing us in no uncertain terms, that there are areas in our make-up which we are powerless to change. One of the more beautiful collects or prayers in the Book of Common Prayer spells out and freely admits to this 'powerlessness', openly acknowledging that 'we have no power of ourselves to help ourselves'. We need to come out of those shadowy illusions where addictive and compulsive patterns of behaviour burgeon, and freely acknowledge our powerlessness, together with the realization that the power to release the human spirit from the bondage and slavery of all addictive behaviour comes alone from God: "'Not by might, nor by power, but by my spirit' says the Lord' (Zechariah 4.6).

Both in the case of addictive and compulsive behaviour as well as in the struggle for freedom from the false self, with its culturally conditioned expectations, we also need to face the painful fact that in many ways we do not want to be free: there is something strangely and powerfully familiar in the habits and ways of the old comfortable self. We are creatures of habit – for better or worse – so that it is a struggle even to want to want release from slavery to the old, familiar and false self, although clearly its continued maintenance requires various crutches and culturally conditioned support systems just to 'keep going'.

So if we are to follow faithfully the spiritual journey from the old to the new and from the false to the true self, we will need to know from the outset that we must let go of the cultural conditioning of *independence*, so much coveted in an age and culture of individualism. Independence will need to be replaced by a total *dependence* upon the work of the Holy Spirit to re-form and recreate us according to the true likeness of the Creator, together with a spirit of *interdependence* with others out on the road of the same spiritual journey. Our membership in the wider community of the Church is as essential for the rebuilding of the new self, as membership in an active cell of Alcoholics Anonymous is to the recovering alcoholic for regaining and maintaining sobriety. Frequently, however, it is only repeated failure on any or many fronts that finally drives us – and then only as a last resort, not unlike the recovering alcoholic – to admit our powerlessness, to reach out and to open up to the higher power of the Holy Spirit. It is at that point and that point only that we validate from our own deep experience the truth in the words of Jesus to his bewildered disciples, that what with man is impossible, with God alone is always possible (Luke 18.27).

In finally coming to that realization, however, we must resist the temptation to despair. Worldly wisdom would naively chorus the old adage that 'the leopard never changes its spots'. Such a hopeless prognosis refutes the possibility of the divine intervention of the transforming power of the Holy Spirit.

Just consider for a moment the unpromising and pathetically unimpressive raw material that was available to Jesus when it came to the choice of those first disciples. Most of the time, the Twelve totally misunderstood most of what Jesus had been teaching them. Even after the resurrection of Jesus and during the farewell encounter with his chosen disciples, all eleven of them were still labouring under the totally wrong impression that Jesus was about to lead a revolution to release the Jews from the Roman occupation. 'Lord, is this the time when you will restore the Kingdom to Israel?' (Acts 1.6). Then again, on the mountain of the Ascension, Matthew records at the end of his Gospel how the 'eleven' (already one short, by the demise of Judas), were gathered to receive their worldwide commission, and yet how, even at this late hour, we are told that some 'still doubted' (Matthew 28.16–20).

The power of the Holy Spirit

Just before his Ascension, Jesus explicitly commands the somewhat pathetic little band of disciples to 'wait', to stay put and 'not to leave Jerusalem, but to wait for the promise of the Father' (Acts 1.4). It is that 'waiting' upon God which should be replicated daily in our times of prayer and with the same expectations of further empowerment as we grow in the life of the Holy Spirit.

Locked in fear as they were, behind closed doors, that first rather broken little band of disciples could not possibly have had any remote idea of how God, through the gift of himself in the Holy Spirit, would transform them and empower them to initiate the greatest revolution the world has ever seen, albeit a very different revolution from the one they had looked to Jesus for on the eve of his Ascension. Mission impossible and highly improbable is wonderfully empowered by the Spirit of the ascended Christ who 'to frail earthen vessels and things of no worth' nevertheless entrusts the riches of his grace, for as St Anselm says, 'Whom he calls, he empowers.'

Paul struggles to make sense of the divine power at work in contradictory situations. From his later experience he testifies that God delights to choose earthen vessels (cracked at that) into which he willingly and generously pours the treasure of himself, and all this so that finally we are compelled to realize our own powerlessness to transform ourselves. 'We have this treasure in clay jars, so that it may be made clear that this extraordinary power belongs to God and does not come from us (2 Corinthians 4.7).

In that self-emptying, God is glorified as we are sanctified. Again, St Paul, with his strong will and intellect, needed to learn the further and most difficult lesson, that it is precisely when we realize our own weakness and acknowledge it, that we are most open to receive the strength and power of God for change and transformation. In the case of Paul, God did not respond to his fervent prayer by taking away that weakness, moral failing or physical impediment – that 'thorn in the flesh' as Paul refers to it. On the contrary, it would seem that Paul's 'problem' was God's opportunity, for Paul was to receive God's power and strength precisely *in* and *through* that self-same weakness. 'My grace is sufficient for you,' the Lord said in response to Paul's prayer, 'for power is made perfect in weakness.' That too should be our experience as we struggle with our inbuilt weaknesses and failings (2 Corinthians 12.9, 10). It's as though grace is the 'joker' in God's pack of cards, which determines that the outcome is an 'all win' situation!

It's the witness of Mary the Mother of the Lord, however, which is most compelling as overwhelming evidence for the power of the Holy Spirit to unite with our spirit in the miracle of the new creation and so to fulfil the promise of making 'all things new'. It was Mary whom God chose as the earthen vessel for the miraculous cosmic turnaround of our redemption – a mere teenage girl from the one-horse town of Nazareth. The invitation of the angel Gabriel for Mary to become the mother of the Chosen One would understandably be perceived at first with total incredulity – with even greater incredulity than when Sarah, in her old age, received a similarly incredible 'annunciation'.

'How can this be, since I know not a man' – that is to say that I am not in a relationship? (Luke 1.34, AV). It was and is a perfectly natural response. Likewise, as I commit myself to a daily time of prayer with the amazing possibility that I can come to know (that is, to be in an intimate relationship with) God. Surely, I must continually be asking myself, 'How can this be, and not least since I am clearly unworthy of such a relationship? Surely this must be the ultimate delusion!'

The response of the angel to Mary's question is good news for her, and at the same time it is good news for the rest of the whole human race, for, as promised by God to the prophet Joel, 'I will pour out my Spirit upon all flesh' (Joel 2.28–32). (It is significant that Peter in the first Christian sermon on the day of Pentecost should put that same text with that same promise as banner headlines in the good news of the day – the birthday of the Christian Church.) So the angel promises the outpouring of that same Holy Spirit to enable Mary to fulfil her unique vocation. 'The Holy Spirit will come upon you and the power of the Most High will overshadow you; so therefore the child to be born will be holy.' Like Mary, we also need to know and to be assured that the 'highest power' – no less than the power of the Holy Spirit, the Spirit of love – can do for us, each in our own particular vocation as the children of God, as that same 'highest power' did for Mary, that which neither we nor her alone could possibly achieve.

So the whole destiny of the human race hangs on two complementary affirmations. The first is the divine promise of the gift of the Holy Spirit – that amazing grace which from all the evidence, it would seem, is assured. The second is a little more problematic. Mary's ultimate response to the divine offer was 'Let it be with me according to your word' – or, in Latin, *'fiat mihi'*, or 'Amen', or just an unqualified 'Yes', or even quite bluntly – 'OK God'! In whatever language or with whatever words – preferably the shorter the better – Mary willingly consented to co-operate for her part in the divine operation to initiate the new creation. This beautiful and lofty disposition of Mary's soul 'is admirably revealed in those simple words *Fiat mihi*. Note how perfectly they agree with those words which our Lord wishes us to have always on our lips and in our hearts: *Fiat voluntas tua*, words from the Lord's own prayer – "*Thy* will be done on earth as it is in heaven".'[1]

Or again, in the Garden of Agony when Jesus himself prays his own prayer to his Father: 'Not what I want, but what you want' (Mark 14.36). As God waited for Mary's affirmative response, so God patiently waits for a similar response from us each and every day, and not only with our lips, but also overflowing from our hearts and eventually spilling over into our everyday lives.

Working together with God

In what ways then, should we speak of passivity in prayer as well as in relation to this whole process of transformation? In the first creation it was God who accomplished everything as a divine fiat, as the Holy Spirit hovered and overshadowed the work of God over the waters of the earth. Dust became clay, and from the clay, God formed Adam.

But it is not so with the new creation. In forming the new creation God calls us to be workers together with him. For humanly speaking, without the consent and co-operation of Mary with her willingness to open herself to the work of God within her, expressed in her consent, and her 'Amen' giving the green light to the divine purposes of God, the new creation would not have been possible. So in the continuing work of the new creation, it would seem that God has chosen not to complete his work 'single-handed', so to speak. Mary had her essential part to play, and so do we in co-operating with the divine plan. It follows therefore that to speak of passivity either in prayer or indeed in anything else in the course of our formation is in danger of reducing spirituality to pietism and quietism, which unlike some Eastern religions, should have no place in Christianity. For in pietism, we leave it all to God. Not so with Christian spirituality. St Augustine gets this balance between the initiative of the divine work and our co-operation with his aphorism: 'Without God, we cannot: without us, he will not.'

The two belong together and work together. Without God there is no way that the new creation could possibly come about. Conversely and at the same time, God has chosen not to bring to birth the new from the old, without our co-operation, though it has to be said that he could have done so, if he had so chosen.

So what about free will and the place of freedom in all of this? Unlike Mary with her uncompromising 'Yes' to God, with most of us, most of the time, it's a question of 'Yes' one minute and 'No' the next. The prayer that can transform us and change us into becoming the people of God, is that in which we willingly place ourselves in the hands of God and consent, like Mary, to give that same green light for the ongoing work of the Holy Spirit to perfect his work in us. In this way the seemingly impossible is possible, as we are made and re-made increasingly into the likeness of God, in which he first created us. Our role in that long and frequently painful process is certainly not passive but rather co-operative as we surrender in a spirit of 'self-abandonment to the divine providence' (de Caussade, the French Jesuit priest and writer).

The potter and the clay

One of the most telling images of this interaction between God the Holy Spirit and each and every human being is to be found in the story of Jeremiah's visit to the potter, following the instructions of the Lord. 'So I went down to the potter's house, and there he was working at his wheel. The vessel he was making of clay was spoiled in the potter's hand, and he reworked it into another vessel, as seemed good to him' (Jeremiah 18.3, 4).

From our point of view, as we pray and live out the spiritual journey, the imagery is quite clear: we are the clay, in the same way that Israel was the clay, with God the Holy Spirit as the potter. 'Behold, like the clay in the potter's hand, so are you in my hand.' Following through the analogy, it is clear that the original vessel was 'spoiled' and malformed and did not work out according to the original design of the potter. Each of us in every generation, just as much as Israel, is the clay in the potter's hands. Clearly, the clay cannot of itself shape itself, even if it ever quite knew what it was ever intended to become. Is it to be a water jar, a beautiful vase or whatever? Its identity, like the identity of all of us, exists in the mind of the 'potter', in whose hands the clay will be moulded, as it seems 'good to him'. All attempts at self re-invention pander only to the old ego with its self-made image, as we discussed earlier, and all attempts at self-formation or reinvention following the analogy of the clay and the potter will necessarily and inevitably prove to be pointless.

> If we want to be anything other than what God has made us to be, we are wasting our time. It will not work. The greatest accomplishment in life is to be what we are, which is God's idea of what he wanted us to be when he brought us into being; and no ideas of ours will ever change it.[2]

These are hard words for self-made men and women, worshipping their maker! So again, we might well ask, 'Where is free will in all of this?', recognizing, as we must, that the initiative is always with God in re-creation as in the first creation. Of itself the clay cannot make anything – all it can do is just spin around on the wheel without direction or formation. The clay only becomes what it was intended to be in the hands of the potter as he works at the wheel.

> The true life of the clay is to spin into symmetry under the maker's hand; yet nothing results, either, by the mere force of the hand, unless the clay is fit and responds. The skill of the divine potter is an infinite patience of improvisation.[3]

It's as though God incorporates the flaws and mistakes in our lives into the ultimate design, improvising infinitely as he continues the work of our salvation. 'No sooner has one work gone awry,' says Austin Farrer, 'than his fingers are pressing it into the form of another.' Like the work of creation, the work of re-creation is ongoing, representing, as it does, the infinite patience of God.

> There is never a moment for the clay when the potter is not doing something with it. God is never standing back and watching us; his fingers are on us all the time. The world is his, from every side he touches and presses us. If we love his will we take the shape of it.[4]

This image of the potter and the clay should help us adjust to the distorted image of what we mean by prayer and indeed the whole of our lives as we pursue the spiritual journey. 'His fingers are on us all the time.' In a real sense, we do not begin or end prayer, properly understood. God for his part is always working in us and with us to perfect what he has first begun. As the psalmist says, 'You press upon me behind and before and lay your hand upon me. I will thank you because I am marvellously made; your works are wonderful and I know it well' (Psalm 139.5, 14). The psalmist was speaking in wonder at the first creation: how much more wonderful is the glory of the new creation!

So we take up our part in God's prayer for us and from our side, as we turn to the Lord and consciously rest in him, consenting and responding to the Holy Spirit who is poured into our hearts whenever we open up to him. But that prayer does not end when we go to our work or our daily life, provided that the repeated affirmations of our prayer time are lived out in our lives – discipleship seen as a repeated consent with its affirming 'Amen' at all times and in all places. 'Every event is a touch of the living finger of God . . . which is sketching within us – body, soul and spirit – the true image of his Son.'[5]

It follows that we should not say 'Yes' in our prayers to God and then 'No' in the subsequent actions of the day, by what we say or by what we do: there is no place for just 'doing our own thing'.

All this work of transformation in God's new creation in us is essentially work in progress, and yet the end product is already in view.

> There is no end indeed to God's making of man. But God has not set the goal of the process in an imaginary future, where we cannot see it. He has set up the goal; it is revealed, it exists, the work has been finished in Christ. What never ends is our receiving the grace of Christ, our growing up into the image of Christ, until we see the face of Christ.[6]

Then we shall know as we are known, and, in knowing God as he truly is, we shall know who we truly were created to be, transformed from one degree of glory to another, reflecting increasingly the divine likeness.

Notes

1 Jean-Pierre de Caussade, *Self Abandonment to Divine Providence* (St Benedict Press Classics, 2006), Book 1, Chapter 1.
2 Thomas Keating, *The Heart of the World: An Introduction to Contemplative Christianity* (Crossroad Publishing, 1981), p. 83.
3 Austin Farrer, *The Essential Sermons: Edited and Introduced by Leslie Houlden* (Cowley Publications, 1991), p. 18.

4   Farrer, *The Essential Sermons.*
5   Farrer, *The Essential Sermons.*
6   Farrer, *The Essential Sermons.*

12

The Freedom of Holiness

Amazing grace

Finding our heart and recovering this awareness of our inmost identity implies the recognition that our external, everyday self is to a great extent a mask and a fabrication. It is not our true self. And indeed our true self is not easy to find.[1]

The spiritual journey as we have written about it in the pages of this book is essentially about the discarding of that fabricated mask of the counterfeit, such as we saw at the outset in the painting by François Lemoyne, together with all the outer wrappings and clothing behind which we all hide to a greater or lesser extent in the quest for that 'true self' which alone can reflect the glory of God in a human being, fully alive and free. Although this process of transformation presupposes our co-operation, we have seen that both the initiative as well as the ability to process this growth from start to finish is primarily the work of God the Holy Spirit. 'For we are what he has made us, created in Christ Jesus for good works, which God prepared beforehand to be our way of life' (Ephesians 2.10). At every turn of the road we need to face up to two overriding imperatives: none of this process of transformation is within our own unaided capabilities; and second, transformation is never fully realized in this world.

St Paul came to the realization that only the grace of God could rescue him from the bondage of sin, deeply imbedded in the false self, as he continually failed to measure up to the requirements of the laws of his religion. 'I can will what is right, but I cannot do it. For I do not do the good I want, but the evil that I do not want is what I do' (Romans 7.18, 19). Was a truer word ever spoken about our human condition? Yet it was the persistent experience of this dilemma which finally drove Paul into the arms of the grace of Christ – arms extended in loving acceptance. So finally he explodes: 'By the grace of God I am what I am' (1 Corinthians 15.10). Grace could do what the law could never do, in the same way that a living faith in the person of Christ has brought to perfection what 'religion' as such can never achieve.

It requires faith and trust in the sufficiency of God's grace and his loving acceptance if we are to persist in our disciplines of discipleship, especially in our commitment to the inner life of personal prayer. The daily life of Christian discipleship is a kind of life betwixt and between, sometimes referred to as holding on to 'the end in the middle'. Such a perspective on life requires what we might want to call a 'bi-focal' attitude to everything. It's as though everything in the 'immediate' must nevertheless be perceived from the perspective of the 'ultimate', whether it be success or failure, loss or gain, sadness or joy. It was precisely this double perspective which enabled Paul to set present hardships and sufferings (to say nothing of his failures and weaknesses) within the bigger picture, leading him to assert with confidence that 'the sufferings of this present time are not worth comparing with the glory about to be revealed to us' (Romans 8.18).

So there is a real tension at the heart of Christian discipleship: a tension between the ultimate ideal and the apparent reality of the present. We know in our heart of hearts the destination of our journey, but equally we know that we still have a long way to travel. The challenge throughout that long journey is to hold realistically with a 'double grip' to a totally realistic self-understanding in the present, and yet at the same time to keep the vision of God's ultimate loving purposes for us – to hold the tension between those two apparently contradictory faces.

> We can cling to some idealistic image of the way human life should be and spin around unsettled all our life. Or we can give up our ideals and settle in the 'real' and live a rather disappointing or maybe even a profoundly disappointed life. Or we can choose to live in the dynamic and exciting tension of a life that clings to an ideal, lovingly embraces the real – in oneself and in others and in all else – and gently moves toward the ideal.[2]

The contemplative life is supremely the way of living with that tension. By and large our present society with its pluralistic culture is no longer willing to live with such a tension. Various brands of so-called 'situational' ethics – whether secular or religious – would firmly insist that we live 'realistically' with the seductive motto: 'Well, after all, we're only human.' Even worse is the temptation to cave in altogether and simply to contend that any ultimate ideal is merely a utopian delusion and that the only realistic way of life is to make the best of a bad job, mainly on our terms and with our best ends in view. Certainly, in essence, that would be the opinion of many who would claim to have 'seen through' – in the worst sense – everything and everybody. When we claim to have seen through everything, however, there are really only two alternatives: cynicism or contemplation. The spirit of cynicism would seem to have won the day, endemic as it is in the world at the present time, best summarized perhaps in John Lennon's lyric: 'Imagine there's no heaven, it's easy if you try.'

Yet it is the contemplative who persists in holding on, in a spirit both of realism and idealism, leaving it to God in the redeeming work of Christ to draw the two together in his time and in his way and with the quiet inner confidence that God's grace is sufficient. Our role in all of this is quite simply to give to God time and space in our lives for those bright beams of his love to draw us from the darkness of the false self into the light of his healing and transforming presence, raising us into a springtime of loving; rather like the sap of trees, with the lengthening days of spring, is drawn upwards – albeit against the force of gravity – to the farthest branches, to the leaves, the blossom and ultimately to the fruits of summer and maturity. Such is what we mean by contemplative living – giving God each and every day the time and space for us to 'rest in his presence' (as Pope Gregory described contemplative prayer) consenting to the transforming power of God's unconditional love.

Goodness and holiness

The ultimate destination of the spiritual journey and the goal of all our true longings, desires and yearnings is nothing less than holiness of life – an authentic life that seeks to speak the 'truth in love' as we 'grow up into Christ' (Ephesians 4.15). Like so much of the vocabulary of all religions – and not least the Christian religion – a word such as 'holiness', through abuse and misuse, caricature and hypocrisy, loses its power to 'connect'.

As we search around for another word to substitute for holiness, there is much talk today of 'wholeness'. To that end, people speak of, and indeed practice various 'meditation techniques' in the belief that 'wholeness' is within our grasp, much like any other product in an acquisitive society. That so-called 'rich young ruler' came to Jesus precisely with such a request – to 'get' and by implication to acquire this product called 'eternal life' that everybody was talking about: 'get a life', as the saying goes, suggesting that it is possible to acquire wholeness much like any other product, off the shelf, if you are 'in the know' as to where to go shopping for it. Yet I would venture to go as far as saying that, if I could attain to psychological, physiological, physical or any other kind of wholeness, I would probably be irredeemable, finally tempted to see the work of grace as little more than an optional extra.

In an age of 'selfism', there are other words which parade as more appropriate and attractive words to substitute for holiness – 'fulfilment' and 'fulfilled'. However, Jesus did not promise fulfilment in the sense that it is used in our day. The danger with being fulfilled by programmes of our own devising, is that we might never reach out to be filled with that life of God that is paradoxically characterized by self-emptying. Jesus, in his teaching as well as in his life, exemplified that quality of life which paradoxically is best expressed through self-emptying. The teaching of Christ insists that it is in self-giving, rather than self-serving, that we receive and are truly fulfilled.

For a holy life (and we should settle for nothing less) is a life that is continually emptied out and poured out for others, as Christ emptied himself in order to be one with us in our human condition. All God's gifts are given to be given away, including life itself. Such is the abundant life of which Jesus speaks. Such a life never runs out, not because it is not being emptied out, but rather because it is being constantly renewed and refilled with the divine life, generously resourced directly from the heart of God himself, the source of 'living water'. This whole divine attitude to life is the very opposite of our contemporary under-standing of wholeness or abundant life in a society that frequently comes to the Christian faith with the same secular attitudes that persist in an acquisitive and self-serving consumerist society.

For the addiction of consumerism is not necessarily restricted to material goods. Without a change of heart and a conversion of life we can be equally consumerist about 'spiritual' goods to bolster the old ego. A generation soured and disillusioned with material consumerism could be only too ready to switch to the supermarket of 'religious options' so evidently on display in our own day.

In his letter to the Ephesians, Paul writes: 'Put away your former way of life, your old self . . . and clothe yourselves with the new self, created according to the likeness of God in true righteousness and holiness' (Ephesians 4.22f). Here again, Eugene Peterson with his paraphrase in *The Message* drives home with vivid clarity the punch of this passage: 'Take on an absolutely new way of life – a God-fashioned life, a life renewed from the inside and working itself into your conduct as God accurately reproduces his character in you.' Such is authentic holiness – 'a God-fashioned life, a life renewed from the inside'.

For there is something authentic and indeed self-authenticating about true holiness of life – something of substance that endures the test of time and change. The counterfeits of holiness are legion and are frequently passed off as the real thing, but only until they stand alongside the genuine article. In his remarkable book, *The Great Divorce*, C. S. Lewis vividly contrasts our transparent and 'hollow' humanity in the process of being redeemed, with the fully redeemed backdrop of the heavenly scene, beyond the grave in a kind of purgatorial hinterland:

At first, of course, my attention was caught by my fellow-passengers . . . I gasped when I saw them. Now that they were in the light, they were transparent – fully transparent when they stood between me and it, smudgy and imperfectly opaque when they stood in the shadow of some tree. They were in fact ghosts: man-shaped stains on the brightness of that air. One could attend to them or ignore them at will as you do with the dirt on a window pane. I noticed that the grass did not bend under their feet: even the dew drops were not disturbed. Then some re-adjustment of the mind or some focusing of my eyes took place, and I saw the whole phenomenon the other way round. The men were as they had always been; as all the men I had known had been perhaps. It was the light, the grass, the trees that were different; made of some different substance, so much more solid than things in our country that men were ghosts by comparison.[3]

Throughout all his writings, Lewis maintains this contrast between the real world of the beyond, and the transparent and ephemeral country of what he calls the 'shadowlands' of this world. Could it be that our celebrity culture at heart is hungry for what dazzles, and so mistakes the spectacular for a transcendence that alone can lift us out of ourselves into a space where there is freedom to grow and to expand and to explore the length and breadth and depth and height of that Love whose name is God?

The freedom to fail

On the spiritual journey there will always be the possibility of failure and apparent disaster. It would seem that in the celebrity culture of our day we cannot handle failure – moral or otherwise. Driven to succeed and the rewards of apparent success, we allow ourselves to be seduced into believing that the show must go on at all costs.

Alas! 'tis true I have gone here and there,
And made myself a motley to the view,
Gored mine own thoughts, sold cheap what is most dear.[4]

However, when failure in any of its many forms and guises overtakes us, we have nowhere to turn and precious few with whom we can honestly share what the experience of failure has done to us. Yet the truth is that we all live in moral glasshouses, fragile and easily shattered by the 'changes and chances' of our human condition. Those very same sins and failings, skids and even crashes in the course of our journeying, can open us up when we have broken down to the miracle of grace and to that transformation of life which is so central to the good news of the gospel. For the test of the true Church is not so much whether or not it can help to make good men and women better, but rather whether it can make bad, fallen, broken and failed men and women holy. Often it is our failures and weaknesses that bring us to that point of reaching out to God for his grace and his loving acceptance.

'Do you turn to Christ?' That is the question addressed to every candidate for baptism. So often and in practice, we only turn to Christ when we find from bitter experience that there is no one else left to whom we can turn. God so often is the last resort in life, for so-called 'death-bed' conversions don't only occur 'in bed' or when we are faced with our imminent mortality. Whenever, however and wherever we turn to the Lord – and not least when we have crashed in failure and disaster – there is a glorious and new opportunity for Christ to enter in and to be with us *in* the pain.

> We must live from our weakness, from the barren places of our need, because there is the spring of grace and the source of our strength . . . For many of us it is difficult to live honestly from this place of failure and weakness. Even if we know with our heads we should, we may slip back into the old attitudes and behave as though God were expecting us to succeed and making his love conditional upon our achievements. If we have become hardened in such an attitude it may take some deep experience of failure to disabuse us.[5]

It is in such experiences of failure when we feel that there is no one to whom we can turn and when yet again we have fallen back into the old habitual and false self – it is at those very times that the Holy Spirit is further released in us for resurrection and new life.

> Here as we teeter on the edge of despair, beset by every kind of temptation and feeling as though we had already fallen,

the Spirit is released. This is his own place, the deepest place of our being where he is wedded to our spirit, where he can act and give life, where he can free us from all that hampers the true thrust of our will. God himself creates our freedom; he gives us freedom as his continuing gift of love, and he alone can influence it from within, in no way violating it or diminishing it. Entombed Lazarus is a sign not simply of a group of people who had obviously closed their hearts against Jesus, but of each one of us. In this hopeless situation, where you are nothing but stark failure, you know the miracle of grace. This tomb is the place of resurrection and if you believe you will see the glory of God.[6]

True freedom

Our ultimate and true identity is revealed to the extent that we have abandoned ourselves to the God who is, in himself, freedom – that freedom of the Spirit which blows where and as it wills, catching us up, taking us out of ourselves and beyond ourselves. If we are to understand prayer properly 'we must see it as our freedom emerging from the depths of our nothingness . . . the flowering of our inmost freedom in response to the Word of God'.[7]

It follows therefore that we cannot assent to the liberating call of God to his people – as in the paradigm of the deliverance of the people of Israel from the bondage of Egypt – if our hearts and minds are still enslaved, continually harking back to the culturally conditioned, false self of our immaturity, with all its hang-ups. Yet as in the same way that the people of Israel could never have broken free from the bondage of Egypt unless God himself had delivered them through his servant Moses, so it is with us and with all our vain attempts at liberation. Freedom, like happiness and joy, is a byproduct of something else – something else that is always essentially beyond. You don't get it by going for it. True freedom, like true love, is within the very

129

nature of who God is – a communion of Persons, existing in the freedom of self-giving love. We only enter into that freedom to the extent that we are in relationship with God. Thomas Merton used to say, 'modern man needs *liberation* from his inordinate self-consciousness, his monumental self-awareness, his obsession with self-affirmation'.[8]

The liberation from self is only possible to the extent that we have lost ourselves in the worship and love of the Other, whose very nature is freedom and love. 'Now the Lord is the Spirit, and where the Spirit of the Lord is, there is freedom' (2 Corinthians 3.17).

Beyond the last horizon

Not that I have already obtained this or am already perfect; but I press on to make it my own, because Christ Jesus has made me his own. Brethren, I do not consider that I have made it my own; but one thing I do, forgetting what lies behind and straining forward to what lies ahead, I press on toward the goal for the prize of the upward call of God in Christ Jesus. Let those of us who are mature be thus minded; and if in anything you are otherwise minded, God will reveal that also to you. Only let us hold true to what we have attained. (Philippians 3.12–16, RSV)

There is something most encouraging about this statement by Paul, written as it is in his last letter from prison, after years of prayer, reflection, ministry and mission in which he admits that he is still out on the road of the spiritual journey and most certainly still not at the finishing post. He tells us in no uncertain terms that he has not got it 'all buttoned up', or 'made it all his own' as yet. His only confidence is that Christ Jesus has made him his own, and that is all he really needs to know if he is to press on toward the ultimate goal of maturity in Christ.

He would freely admit that he does not need to know at this point what the contours and scenery of the land of promise will look like, nor even what he will look like at the end of the journey. At this point, all such details are beyond the horizon of our limited understanding. All he and we need to know as we travel, is that when we reach the finishing post, as St John assures us, we shall see the face of God and will be truly like him, reflecting that likeness yet in our own unique personhood.

We shall know who we were truly created to be – namely, partakers of the divine life, lived within the freedom of true Love and sharing in the divine life of the Blessed Trinity. All this is possible and indeed is the basis of Christian hope in a world that appears to be so very far from any kind of meaning or maturity or indeed the freedom that only true holiness of life can bring. It is possible because it is with and from God from start to finish and not by any self-righteousness on our part. It is God's own 'divine power that has granted to us all things that pertain to life and godliness, through the knowledge of' (that is, by being in this deep relationship through the inner life of prayer and worship) 'him who called us to his own glory and excellence' to 'become partakers of the divine nature' (2 Peter 1.4).

So it is that the Fathers of the Church speak unapologetically of our ultimate goal as being divinized. As the human story unfolds and when all at last is said and done, we shall be able to rejoice paradoxically in the Fall of Adam ('O happy sin of Adam' as St Augustine refers to the fall of Man) or rather in what God has been able to do with the fundamental flaw in the whole of his creation. For Adam's creation before the Fall can now be seen retrospectively as being only 'second best'. After all, according to scripture, he was created 'a little lower than the angels'. The Second Adam – the ascended Christ, and we together with him and in him – have been raised above the angels (Hebrews 1.4f.) into the heart of the Triune God.

In order to love God truly we must, as incredible as it seems to say it, be made divine. We cannot do it ourselves. If we are to be divine, to be made perfect as the Father is perfect, it can only be because God dwells in us and works our transformation . . . So we can see that the Lord is not merely teaching us that he is boss in order to assert his authority, his lordship . . . If that were true we would still be servants and the whole purpose of our prayer life would be to affirm and re-enforce our servitude. There are great religions in which this vision of God and man prevails, but Christianity is not one of them. Rather, the reason for our loving surrender to God is that we desire to be able to love as we are loved, and only the Lord can effect in us the transformation which this demands.[9]

Notes

1   Thomas Merton, *The Climate of Monastic Prayer* (Irish University Press, 1969), p. 97.
2   M. Basil Pennington, *Aelred of Rievaulx: The Way of Friendship* (New City Press, 2001), p. 11.
3   C. S. Lewis, *The Great Divorce* (Macmillan Publishing Co., 1946), p. 27.
4   Shakespeare, Sonnet 110.
5   Maria Boulding, *Gateway to Hope: An Exploration of Failure* (Collins Fount Paperbacks, 1985), p. 109.
6   Boulding, *Gateway to Hope*, p. 110.
7   M. Basil Pennington, *Thomas Merton, Brother Monk: The Quest for True Freedom* (Harper & Row, 1987), p. 28.
8   Pennington, *Thomas Merton, Brother Monk*, p. 23.
9   Thomas H. Green, SJ, *When the Well Runs Dry: Prayer Beyond the Beginnings* (Ave Maria Press, 1979), p. 104f.

APPENDIX A

'Lectio Divina': A Traditional and Alternative Method of Bible Reading

The Word and the words

The traditional and alternative method of reading scripture, known since the earliest times as *'lectio divina'* or 'spiritual reading', derives its authority from the theological conviction that there is a direct connection between the living Word of God – Jesus 'the Word made flesh' – and the written and inspired words of scripture. This connection is made possible by the work of the Holy Spirit – that self-same Spirit that inspired the words of scripture, and who also indwells the one who is reading scripture.

'All scripture is inspired by God' – 'breathed into' by God with the breath of the Holy Spirit (2 Timothy 3.16). Allied to this text is the promise of Jesus himself, that the Holy Spirit would take the words and teachings of Jesus and re-present them to us – recall them into the present, not simply as words spoken, recorded and written down in the past, but as living words eternally present. In this way the Holy Spirit makes Jesus truly present – the living Word of God who speaks to us *through* the words of scripture. Indeed, such a theology of 'spiritual reading' permits us to speak of the real presence of Jesus, when the word is 'broken open', in a similar way to that in which we speak of the real presence of Jesus when the bread of the Eucharist is 'broken'.

We need to take note of the way in which Jesus revealed himself through both the breaking of the word and the breaking of the bread to those first two disciples on the road to Emmaus, when 'he interpreted to them in all the scriptures the things concerning himself' (Luke 24.27). In other words, the scriptures only 'come alive' when they relate directly to Jesus the Word made flesh, who is Lord of scripture as he is Lord of the Church. Jesus himself said to his disciples, 'I have said these things to you while I am still with you. But the Advocate, the Holy Spirit, whom the Father will send in my name, will teach you every-thing, and remind you of all that I have said to you' (John 14.25, 26). It's as though the written words of scripture are customized, personalized and made contemporary.

> The danger for us, with our critical minds, is that the text will become a history book, even though God is its protago-nist and its subject is his marvels. For the ancients, 'the text breathes'. Beneath its formulas they saw his mysterious presence. Scripture is God present who speaks to me. More precisely, when I go beyond the letter of Scripture to its spirit, I personally encounter the living Christ. He is present to explain his own Word which is gradually revealed to the eyes of faith.[1]

So in this alternative approach to the reading of scripture, we are not so much seeking further knowledge about God, but rather using the God-given and inspired words of scripture to deepen our relationship with God, which is a rather different kind of knowledge. Indeed, 'information knowledge' through the processes of the mind can actually hinder or even block the way to that 'knowledge of the heart' of which Pascal speaks, which kindles an experience of the Other, as those two disciples rightly admitted: 'Were not our hearts burning within us while he was talking to us on the road, while he was opening the scriptures to us?' (Luke 24.32) – an experience further endorsed in a complementary exercise recorded later in that same chapter, when the risen Lord subsequently 'opened their minds' to the scriptures. Both these exercises are required – the 'opening' of the scriptures together with the 'opening' of hearts and minds to *receive* God's living, contemporary Word – and all this, from start to finish, the continuing work of the Holy Spirit.

> The Spirit whom Jesus promised the Father would send in his name to dwell within us, is the same Spirit who vivifies the word of scripture. It is my active *faith* in this Spirit, present in the word *and* in me, which, when brought to the reading and hearing of scripture, 'in-spires' or 'breathes into' it the living reality of the Speaker.[2]

The practice of reading scripture and listening to the word of God

1. **Preparation** Behind closed doors, away from the telephone or the mobile and where you are not likely to be interrupted, alone and in silence together with the scriptures, sit with a straight back in an attitude of attention and expectation. All this to anticipate the presence of the One who calls me to open my heart and mind to him. In the stillness, perhaps with a short prayer, invoke the Holy Spirit. This is the moment when, as St Jerome said, I 'unfurl my sails to the Holy Spirit'.

2. **Reading a passage of scripture** Read the chosen passage, slowly, attentively and preferably aloud (as St Augustine suggests), and not just once, but also a second time and possibly even a third time. Before we begin to reflect on the passage we need to listen to it and to *receive* it – taking it in, as we say. St Ambrose tells us that we should 'read the words not in agitation, but in calm; not hurriedly, but slowly, a few

at a time, pausing in attentive reflection'. Then, he says, 'the reader will experience the ability to enkindle the ardour of prayer'.

3. **From listening to receiving**   God said to Ezekiel, 'All my words that I shall speak to you receive in your heart' (Ezekiel 3.10). It was in her heart that Mary pondered the words of Jesus and kept them in her heart. Augustine speaks of the 'ears of the heart' and even of the 'mouth of the heart', comparing meditation to the assimilation of food, as the psalmist exhorts: 'Taste and see that the Lord is good.' The more the word of God is 'chewed' in the mouth, the more sweetly it is savoured in the heart. Only in this way are the analytical processes of the mind bypassed, as the centre of consciousness moves from head to heart.

4. **Meditation**   Now put the scriptures to one side because, perhaps by this stage, a short phrase has sprung from the text and can be translated into a short prayer to God. Conversely, a phrase may have a new and personal significance in the light of present circumstances. Then again, meditation or mental prayer conjures up a picture of an event based on the passage. When this occurs we can sometimes put ourselves in the place of one of the characters in the story, approaching Jesus in the same way as the younger son approached his father in the parable of the Prodigal Son, for example, or even assume the role of the elder brother.

In this way when the Word of God has taken root in our hearts, the seat of all our desires and longings, then we are drawn away from the written words to the Person in dialogue.

Express to God in the simplest way the impression the words have made on you. You may want to thank God for the gift they convey, ask the questions they have stirred in you, put into words the longings or needs they have brought up. Keep it simple, praying spontaneously. Or you may want to respond by simply remaining in loving silence in the presence of God.[3]

5. **An open-ended conclusion** When and how we close these times of meditation and prayer should be seen as open-ended. Sometimes, God graces us in a very special way and we find ourselves attracted and drawn very close to the Lord – a little like the quivering needle in a compass seeks to 'find' the north, as we move more into contemplative prayer, the wordless prayer of silence, without images – sometimes called the 'prayer of loving regard'. Gregory the Great speaks of these graced times of prayer quite simply as 'resting in God'. (For more about this and Centering Prayer, see Appendix B.)

6. Then again, you may wish to bring your prayer time to a close with prayers of thanksgiving, a well-known prayer and/or the Lord's Prayer and possibly the Grace.

In all of this however, we need to be free to follow the Spirit with the two provisos. All the spiritual writers are adamant in the need to submit ourselves to a wise spiritual director. 'Resist not the Spirit' but conversely, 'Test the Spirits to see if they are of God.' The gift and practice of discernment is essential if we are to go deeper into the life of prayer, because the deeper we go, the more we are open to delusion and fantasy.

And second, a wise spiritual director will know of that over-riding advice of Dom Chapman, a famous Benedictine spiritual director of the early part of the twentieth century, when he said, 'Pray as you can, not as you can't', for when it comes to deep prayer we are all novices and beginners.

For the simplest of words, when genuine and sincere – or even no words at all when the heart is too full – are surely more eloquent than the most lyrical rhetoric which is fabricated or borrowed.[4]

'Lectio divina', often translated as 'spiritual reading', means not only reading the text but also meditating on the text, praying the text and living the text. It is reading that enters our souls the way food enters our stomachs, spreads through our blood, and transforms us. Christians don't simply learn or study or use scripture; we feed on it. We assimilate it, taking it into our lives in such a way that it is metabolized into acts of love, cups of cold water, missions into all the world, healing and evangelism and justice in Jesus' name, hands raised in adoration to the Father, feet washed in the company of the Son.[5]

So in this way, we become by the grace of God, doers of the Word, and not merely hearers. (James 1.22)

Notes

1   Mariano Magrassi, *Praying the Bible: An Introduction to Lectio Divina* (Liturgical Press, 1998), p. 21.
2   Thelma Hall, *Too Deep for Words: Rediscovering Lectio Divina* (Paulist Press, 1988), p. 36.
3   Martin L. Smith, *The Word is Very Near You: A Guide to Praying with Scripture* (Cowley Publications, 1989), p. 120.
4   Hall, *Too Deep for Words*, pp. 40–1.
5   Eugene Peterson, *'Conversations': The Message Bible with its Translator* (NavPress, 2005), p. 12.

APPENDIX B

The Practice of Centering Prayer

'For God alone my soul in silence waits.' (Psalm 62)

From conversation to communion

Most of us were brought up to believe that prayer was our way of expressing to God our thankfulness, petitions, needs and concerns in words – or, as we often put it, as 'saying our prayers'. But as we grow and deepen our relationship with God, by the Holy Spirit, we are drawn to move from words to silence, and from a conversational mode into something which is perhaps best described as 'communion' with God. As we open our minds and our hearts to the presence of God within us, we move beyond thinking, with its images and attempts to conceptualize God, seeking only to rest in his presence as prayer increasingly becomes much more what God does in and through us by his Holy Spirit. For our part, we need only to consent to what God wishes to do in us and for us, consenting to the transforming power of the Holy Spirit. So, in God's time and in God's way, we are increasingly set free from the expectations and motivations of the false self and re-created into the new self, reflecting both the likeness as well as the image in which God first created us.

Sometimes it is helpful to begin such times of prayer with the practice of the spiritual reading of a passage of scripture as described in Appendix A – 'lectio divina' – preparing us to listen to God through the words of the scriptural passage as we have read, marked, learned and 'inwardly digested' it.

Beyond words, thoughts and images

With open hearts and open minds, in the silence and in the presence of God, we consent to the work of the Holy Spirit who searches the heart in the depths beneath all the superficialities of the everyday self that we project to the world. Inevitably, as we do this, wandering thoughts of all kinds come up to invade our consciousness. We should neither aggressively suppress these thoughts nor chase them. Rather, we seek to let go of them by gently reasserting our will and our desire to remain open and silent for the continuing work of the Holy Spirit, who is praying in us and for us to the Father.

The prayer word or sacred word

We best reassert our wish to let go of any thoughts or images with the use of a 'sacred word' or words which we repeat as a sign of our willingness and consent to what God is 'praying' and working within us. In choosing the sacred word of consent we should seek the Holy Spirit as a guide, and once we have chosen the word we should stick with it. Any or none of the following words may be used: 'Jesus', 'Lord Jesus', 'Father', 'Abba' or even 'peace', 'trust', 'silence'. The word will be given.

So, as the wandering thoughts or other images come up, we gently reassert our consent to the action of the Holy Spirit by quietly repeating the word (See Chapter 10).

Discipline and commitment

If we are to grow in this practice of Centering Prayer we will need to commit to set times each day. Preferably early in the morning, before the business of the day, and for not less than twenty minutes, we pull aside into an 'inner chamber', shut the door, sitting upright and relaxed. As this becomes part of our daily routine, we will find ourselves extending the time possibly to thirty minutes and possibly again in the evening. In any event, we need to commit with regularity to the pursuit of our spiritual health in much the same way as many people commit to working out in the gym for what they believe to be the good of their physical health. (Incidentally, it is sometimes helpful to set something like a kitchen timer so that we are not tempted to think, 'How much longer have I got!' In practice, sometimes the twenty or thirty minutes seem simply to fly by, or even of course the very opposite. But that does not need to be our concern.)

For encouragement in this practice of Centering Prayer, it can be of help to belong to a small group of people who meet once a week to follow this practice together or to belong to one or other Centering Prayer Fellowships. (See below for further details of such groups).

Further reading on the practice of Centering Prayer

Anthony Bloom, *Living Prayer* (Darton, Longman & Todd, 1966).

Sister Ruth Burrows, *Essence of Prayer* (Burns & Oates, Continuum, 2006).

Thomas H. Green SJ, *When the Well Runs Dry: Prayer Beyond the Beginnings* (Ave Maria Press, 1979).

Kenneth Leech, *True Prayer* (Sheldon Press, 1980).

Henri Nouwen, *The Way of the Heart: Desert Spirituality and Contemporary Ministry* (HarperCollins, 1981).

Elizabeth Smith and Joseph Chalmers, *A Deeper Love: An Introduction to Centring Prayer* (Continuum, 1999).

A selection of works by Thomas Keating

Published by the Continuum International Publishing Group:

Open Mind, Open Heart

Invitation to Love

The Better Part

Published by the Crossroad Publishing Company:

Awakenings

The Heart of the World

Intimacy with God

Published by Paulist Press:

The Human Condition: Contemplation and Transformation

See also: *The Daily Reader for Contemplative Living: Excerpts from the Works of Father Thomas Keating*, compiled by S. Stephanie Iachetta (Continuum, 2007).

For support and further help

Contemplative Outreach UK
Networking; assistance and support in establishing local Centering Prayer programmes; books, audio and video tapes; newsletter; Centering Prayer retreat director.

Contact: The Director, Contemplative Outreach UK, Tree Tops, Houghton Lane, Nr Preston, Lancashire, PR5 4ED.

SPA Fellowship

SPA (Scripture, Prayer and Action) – a fellowship for spiritual refreshment and renewal, committed to times of silent corporate prayer, issuing from a programme of Bible study and leading to action, witness and service. It is the strong conviction of the SPA ministry that such a cell of men and women in all the churches can make a difference at a time of crisis, for both the Church as well as for society. Open churches need open hearts – hearts open to the transforming power of the Holy Spirit at work in the heart of cities and communities everywhere.

For further information, see www.spapray.org.uk.

CD: *More Prayer Songs* by the Revd Soon Han Choi, available from the SPA website.

1348352R0

Printed in Great Britain by
Amazon.co.uk, Ltd.,
Marston Gate.